PASSION-DRIVEN EDUCATION

HOW TO USE YOUR CHILD'S INTERESTS TO IGNITE A LIFELONG LOVE OF LEARNING

CONNOR BOYACK

Libertas Press
SALT LAKE CITY, UTAH

Libertas Press
785 East 200 South, Suite 2
Lehi, UT 84043

Passion-Driven Education: How to Use Your Child's Interests to Ignite a Lifelong Love of Learning

ISBN-13 978-1-943521-11-1 (paperback)

10 9 8 7 6 5 4 3 2

For bulk orders, send inquires to info@libertasutah.org.

CONTENTS

Other titles by the author:

*Feardom: How Politicians Exploit Your Emotions
and What You Can Do to Stop Them*

*Lessons from a Lemonade Stand: An Unconventional
Guide to Government*

The Tuttle Twins children's book series

Anxiously Engaged: Essays on Faith, Family, & Freedom

*Latter-day Responsibility: Choosing Liberty
through Personal Accountability*

*Latter-day Liberty: A Gospel Approach to
Government and Politics*

To my parents

*For providing me with
a solid foundation*

"It is, in fact, nothing short of a miracle that the modern methods of instruction have not yet entirely strangled the holy curiosity of inquiry; for this delicate little plant, aside from stimulation, stands mainly in need of freedom; without this it goes to wreck and ruin without fail. It is a very grave mistake to think that the enjoyment of seeing and searching can be promoted by means of coercion and a sense of duty."

—ALBERT EINSTEIN

FOREWORD

P*assion-Driven Education* is a radical book—radical in the best sense of the basic meaning, that it gets to the heart of an important idea, gets to its essence, gets to its fundamental core. This book explores the root dynamic that makes education superior to schooling: that free-will students do much better than command-education, rule-driven students do. Connor Boyack's book will introduce you to a profound, fundamental truth which we all deeply understand from our early experience, but which professional, institutionalized school personnel *are ordered to forget* in one of the most bizarre chapters of civilized history on record—that we learn much better those things we *choose to learn* through exercise of our free will and through methods in close harmony with our inner nature, instead of through orders from total strangers called schoolteachers, who are given authority over our lives and minds. The founding principles of America are grounded in this truth about the power of liberty.

Take a deep breath now and prepare for an ugly shock: mass institutional schooling is not an "American" invention at all, nor was the intention of its Prussian German creators to educate. The actual purpose, as we learn from an important book written in 1906 by America's first official Commissioner of Education, William Torrey Harris, titled *The Philosophy of Education*, is to "alienate" children from their own natures, from their parents, from their cultures, and from religion, by directly indoctrinating inexperienced young minds under the total control of royal hirelings of the political state called schoolteachers and to psychologically condition students to give unquestioning obedience to politicians alone. They were to be psychologically "conditioned" to develop as political power elites commanded, not to receive competent intelligence at all. *Blind obedience training* is the very purpose of government schooling. As we learn from Prussian philosopher Johann Fichte's 1807 *Second Address to the German Nation*, or Alexander Inglis' 1918 *Principles of Secondary Education*, the purpose was to create an obedient underclass without the skills to rebel.

How this weird perversion of education occurred is fascinating. We know exactly *when* and *where* it happened and *why*. Its record exists in every library, if you know where to look.

In 1806, the tiny North German state of Prussia was a very successful, world-famous military dictatorship, with an economy built around war-making and the renting of soldiers to other war-making nations (including *both* sides in the American Revolution). Prussia's armies were highly professionalized and, according to the *Encyclopedia Britannica* (11th Edition), were able to fire five shots from muzzle-loaded rifles when opponents could only fire two. In Prussia *all* human behavior was under the control of authorities.

Prussia despised the concept of free will for common citizens; free will makes for bad soldiers. The entire civilized world recognized Prussia as the standard model of supreme military excellence; its discipline was superb. Over time, however, discipline among the soldiers began to decline. In 1806, Napoleon defeated Prussia in the catastrophic Battle of Jena, provoking hysteria among Prussia's elite and a near-collapse of its high military reputation.

Who would now want to rent Prussian mercenaries after this military debacle?

The Prussian King and his generals decided that the loss had been caused by common soldiers "thinking for themselves" and deciding which orders to follow and which official commands to obey. Lack of discipline had ruined Prussia at Jena. A new system had to be reconstructed to end free will initiative among the young.

The scholars of Prussia, under a famous philosopher named Johann Fichte, were ordered to invent a scheme to end any possibility of disobedience among the young and new common classes. The result was the very first system in world history for universal institutionalized compulsory schooling as an exclusive monopoly of the political state. Johann Fichte announced this—explaining its purpose explicitly—in a series of public speeches, collected in book form as *Addresses to the German Nation*. Appearing in the first two decades in the 19th century, word of this unique new school institution and its advantages for kings, generals, bosses, and managers spread instantly to every corner of the world (including to America), and plans were made everywhere, by every important nation on earth, to imitate Prussia. Prussian *obedience schooling* became the world standard for official education.

Fichte's book is readily available in American libraries, translated into English. Making thoughtless automatic obedience the end point of education, in service to every kind of authoritarian hierarchy, requires that students be deprived of the capacity to think independently, that they be divorced from learning, and that they give up "critical thinking" as we know it today. Rhetoric and dialectics, which had been the foundation of fine education since the days of ancient Greece, were omitted from the new form of forced school training.

So, after Fichte, mind control of students was the very point of school training—a purpose popular among political leaders, military commanders, and corporate executives, along with bankers and financial interests, because mind control promised that hierarchies of privilege would remain undisturbed for all the future, thus stabilizing the social order. This was a dream of philosophers since Plato, and a fond wish of crony capitalists, who worried about risks to capital investment in a dynamic society without competing class divisions. School freezes the "haves" and "have-mores" at the pinnacle of power by "dumbing down" the common classes, rendering them incompetent. Whether you consider that hypothesis as good or bad depends upon your personal philosophies regarding liberty and self-sovereignty.

Put as a question, are societies and individuals better off in "free" societies, where free will is respected, or in those where commands from "elites" write the script for all? At bottom, this is the profound question considered in *Passion-Driven Education*. Mr. Boyack answers, as most of us would by intuition, in favor of free will, personal choice training, and personal liberty—the same choice America's founders made with the Declaration of Independence. How well you understand this debate depends upon the extent to which you cherish liberty as a human value. But this is a choice negated by the Prussian system of schooling that despises free will in students.

The first serious treatment of education in the Western world was written by the legendary philosopher Plato around 300 B.C. in his dialogue *The Republic*. Plato asked the same question Mr. Boyack does, arriving at the same conclusion. As in his later book *The Laws*, he established education as the path to social perfection in a Greek world which sought wisdom, courage, temperance, and justice. Plato places the debate in *The Republic* between a gentleman named Thrasymachus (who champions Prussia-like strong-state domination) and two younger contestants: Glaucon and Adeimantus (who argue, in effect, that citizens given a right to choose what they learn and how they learn it have more passion for learning and do it better, more thoroughly than those who follow orders from "experts" appointed to command them).

The secret of Greek superiority over Egypt and Persia in the ancient world, according to Plato, was its commitment to personal liberty and *choice in learning* while Egyptians and Persians dictated fields of study. But the bitter irony is that Plato wanted that liberty for all, rich or poor. The idea, as it passes from Greek Plato to Roman Cicero in *De Republica*, to Augustine's *City of God*, to Thomas Moore's *Utopia*, and to other educational authorities down to us in the modern world, is this: what Plato meant as an educational method *for all* has been preserved by elite private boarding schools like Groton, Choate Rosemary Hall, St. Paul's, Milton, and Sidwell Friends, as the exclusive property of wealthy children—a sad reality and ultimate irony.

Mr. Boyack effectively resurrects an ancient idea of libertarian education cherished through millennia by the powerful families of history in every corner of the earth. These principles have been preserved exclusively for their own children, who are destined to inherit management of the future, by equipping them to learn through the freedom granted them to self-educate more than the children of lowly classes who are taught by "workbooks", "standardized" orders, tests, bells, gold stars, and threats which associate learning with stress and the suppression of free will.

I spent three decades as an award-winning, certified public schoolteacher in the Prussian compulsory system, imposing mind control on my students. But in mid-career, facing children "dumbed down" by this methodology I was ordered to impose, I repented.

For the last 20 years of my career, I passionately imitated the libertarian principles existing in elite private boarding schools (where parents are charged upwards of $50,000 a year), and was dazzled by the positive changes in my largely poverty-stricken classes. Awakened to aspiration-driven self-education that directly addressed their own needs, imperatives, and characters, in place of schooling by the injunctions of strangers, my students, thus taught, blossomed in front of my eyes.

Following that Platonic-Augustinian-Ciceronian methodology, I won the New York City Teacher of the Year title three consecutive times, and ended my career as New York State Teacher of the Year in 1991. The mantra that guided my award-winning teaching was: "You need experiences and adventures and explorations more than you need algebra." This is the glorious secret Connor Boyack seeks to share with you in this book if you can abandon your skepticism long enough to try it. Passion-driven education works. You must *aspire* to it! As a philosopher once put it: "Nobody can give you an education; only a schooling can be given. Education must be *taken*."

For best results, parents and teachers must inspire passion in learners by returning choice to them, creating an aspiration to learn. Your own experience will tell you that Connor Boyack's system is the right path to travel. Read this text closely; take its principles to heart. You will be delighted with the positive difference they make to the young you seek to educate. His example, mine, Plato's, Augustine's, and Cicero's should reassure you in deviating from the straightjacket common schooling would have you wear.

John Taylor Gatto
June 2016

PREFACE

Being the author of several successful books, people often assume that I studied in school what I now write and teach about: political philosophy, history, and economics. I chuckle at this assumption, because not only is it untrue, but it completely contradicts my reality.

A few years ago, my mother ran into one of my high school English teachers. My mother informed this teacher—who remembered me well, which is probably a bad thing—that I was now an accomplished author and writing prolifically as part of my full-time profession as the head of a political think tank, Libertas Institute. The teacher was astounded to learn this, because I had been anything but a star student in her class.

Here's the thing: I hated English class. Economics and history were similarly loathsome to me, and I didn't enjoy or perform well in any of these subjects during high school or college. So, perhaps you can see why my English teacher would be surprised to hear a young man had transitioned from writing unintelligible, awkwardly constructed essays to writing an array of books that other people are actually willing to pay to read.

The pertinent question is: how did this happen? How did I come to love and excel in the very subjects that I detested during my school years? More importantly, how can you, as a parent, learn from my own—and, dare I say, my parents'—mistakes? How can you inspire a love of learning in your child, even in subjects that may seem daunting, boring, or irrelevant?

The answer: *freedom.*

Don't write this answer off as trite or simplistic, because, as you'll come to realize by the end of this book, there are substantive and compelling reasons to base our educational approach upon the philosophy of freedom and plenty of practical ways to apply it to every subject under the sun. As we go along, I will provide specific examples to help you understand how allowing your children the freedom to gain an education by pursuing their passions will restore and revitalize their natural desires to learn.

When I graduated from college, I was finally free from all of the exams, projects, and homework that were more of a hindrance than a help toward achieving my goals. I was no longer required to "learn" facts and figures that had no apparent relevance or interest to me, only to regurgitate them for a grade and, inevitably, to forget them soon after. Once I obtained my degree, I had more free time than ever before and the ability to focus my time and mental energy on things which mattered to me. Finally, I had freedom.

So, I read—slowly at first. After so many years of studying what others had chosen on my behalf, my curiosity muscles had atrophied. I soon found that as I read the books I wanted, my curiosity began to grow, and so, I read some more. In 2005, I began to blog about what I was learning and gained a growing readership. That audience made me keenly aware of how *awful* I was at writing; reviewing what I wrote back then is painful for me now. But my embarrassment became an internal motivation to improve. I now had a compelling reason to learn how to write well.

To do so, I didn't crack open my English textbook from college. (Actually, like most students, I sold that ten-pound paperweight as soon as I could.) I didn't begin a technical review of the semantic structure of persuasive writing, fretting over compound pluperfect subjunctives and other mind-numbing minutiae. Instead, I observed and imitated. I read material from authors who wrote well, and I made their practices my own until it became natural for me to communicate well, too. I learned by doing, guided by those who were masters of their craft.

Today, my interests and expertise are in the very subjects which I suffered through in school. It was the freedom to pursue these areas of study on my own terms which inspired me to actively pursue the information I had previously deemed to be useless and dull. This freedom to seek knowledge, once I fully grasped its relevance, opened up a new world to me—one that has turned into a fulfilling career allowing me to influence the lives of tens of thousands of other people.

I offer the foregoing information about myself in order to explain why I believe so passionately that a child's freedom to pursue their individual interests is the most effective way to help them become educated adults because—let's be honest—all lasting education is self-motivated. We cannot compel a person to learn anything. Children who are forced to learn undesired information will allow it to slip from their memory, if they ever learned it at all. As the saying goes, "A man convinced against his will is of the same opinion still."

I believe the most effective and natural form of education is one that centers on the interests of the individual. Find a child's passion, and learning will transition from a chore to a joy. Help them find purpose and meaning in what they are learning, and education loses all of the drudgery, compulsion, and stress that too many parents dismiss as the acceptable collateral damage of the learning process.

A child's curiosity and natural desire to learn are like a tiny flame, easily extinguished unless protected and given fuel. This book will help you as a parent both protect that flame of curiosity, and supply it with the fuel necessary to make it burn bright throughout your child's life.

Let's ignite our children's natural love of learning!

"The aim of [the modern education system] is simply to reduce as many individuals as possible to the same safe level, to breed and train a standardized citizenry, to put down dissent and originality."[1]

—H.L. MENCKEN

ONE

———⊸⊸⊸———

WHAT'S THE PROBLEM?

Education, as it's commonly implemented and understood, is an absolute disaster. I make that unqualified statement based upon a mountain of evidence, some of which we'll discuss in this book. Whether your children are in a government school, private school, or home school, there are a number of problems you'll experience—problems that may suppress, and potentially extinguish, your child's natural desire to learn.

Each child is, by nature, a curious creature. A baby's brain development is astonishingly accelerated; from the moment of conception, the neurons in a baby's brain multiply faster than any other type of cell. By age three, a child's brain has developed so quickly that it has already grown to 90% of its final adult weight. Constantly observing their surroundings, and imitating what they see as best they can, babies are inherently enthralled by the world around them. Every new stimulus is an opportunity to explore and learn.

Now, imagine an average teenager: apathetic, uninvolved, disinterested, and complaining about overwhelming amounts of homework that encroaches upon their limited free time. For too many, their natural desire to learn has been turned into a chore that breeds resentment and disdain. How can this outcome be explained? Why do so many children go from absorbing information to becoming resistant to it? More importantly, how can we learn from and avoid this trend with our own children?

The first thing we need to do is recognize that *education does not equate to school*; the former is not bound by buildings, schedules, and formalized instruction. Too many people have so conflated the two in their minds, and thus in their homes, that learning and instruction are confined to the hours dedicated to formal schooling. Children are being raised to perceive their free time and personal interests as separate from and unrelated to their education. If parents don't emphasize education outside of structured schooling, then should we really expect children to do so?

One of the things I remember most about school was looking at the clock, counting down the minutes until class time was over. The segmentation of education—treating it as something to be scheduled and structured—has conditioned children to see learning as a chore. The system teaches them that if they suffer a little longer, they will earn a few minutes to visit with friends, grab a snack, or listen to some music. The psychological effects of this are unavoidable; by withholding freedom until class is over or an assignment is complete, we instill in our children the idea that learning is a hindrance.

Most children are subjected to coercive methods of education, as described above. They are told *what* to study, *when*, and, in most cases, *where*. When they ask *why*, their teacher may reply, "You have to," or, "It's the law," while a parent might say, "Because I said so," or the rarely true "Because someday you'll need to know it." Coercion in education even bleeds into the *how*, with faceless curriculum committees and unelected bureaucrats deciding the form in which information will be taught, how learning will be assessed, and what methodologies will be allowed.

Coercion—the opposite of freedom—is the root of many of the problems of modern education. To solve these problems, and spare our children from their harmful effects, we must first understand how coercion has come to have such a negative impact on so many aspects of education. A brief analysis of these effects will help us understand why passion-driven education, which will be explained later in detail, can help us heal the harm coercion has caused.

CRAMMING INFORMATION

Ben Orlin is a high school math teacher in Oakland, California. When he addressed the assembled students in his first-ever trigonometry class, he asked them what the sine of π/2 is. Their unified answer, "One!" indicated that they had already covered the material. "We learned that last year," they told their teacher.

Like any new teacher, Orlin zipped ahead through the material, but came to realize that the students didn't really know what "sine" actually meant—they had merely memorized the answer to the question. "To them," Orlin writes, "math wasn't a process of logical discovery and thoughtful exploration. It was a call-and-response game. Trigonometry was just a collection of non-rhyming lyrics to the lamest sing-along ever."

Imagine yourself as a math teacher, or as a parent trying to teach trigonometry to a teenager. Chances are, you're going to rely upon a textbook or some other form of curriculum to do the teaching for you. Your student will be expected to absorb the information presented in the book, and so, he or she packs away that tidbit in the back of his or her brain: the sine of π/2 is one. However, as Orlin notes, this information-heavy approach to education is not ideal:

> Some things are worth memorizing—addresses, PINs, your parents' birthdays. The sine of π/2 is not

among them. It's a fact that matters only insofar as it connects to other ideas. To learn it in isolation is like learning the sentence "Hamlet kills Claudius" without the faintest idea of who either gentleman is—or, for that matter, of what "kill" means. Memorization is a frontage road: It runs parallel to the best parts of learning, never intersecting. It's a detour around all the action, a way of knowing without learning, of answering without understanding.[2]

Regurgitation of information gives the appearance of knowledge mastery while masking the reality of poor comprehension. It's a way for a child to falsely demonstrate retention without having to achieve comprehension. When this onslaught of information is directed at children, the tests are sure to follow.

Remember when you were a student? Part of the experience was *cramming*—spending hours before an exam pushing as much information as possible into our brains, in the hopes that one of the factoids happened to be what the teacher wanted to quiz us on. Sometimes we were allowed to use notes or a small "cheat sheet," leading to minuscule text being packed into the limited space so as to maximize one's chance of success.

Is that education? Is it how you want your child to explore the world and acquire knowledge? Is it healthy? Is it effective? These are some of the most basic questions we can ask, yet if we ask them sincerely, the answers are plainly obvious. Why, then, do we do it? Peter Kaufman, a professor of sociology at the State University of New York, observed:

> As a college professor, I see the dysfunctional effects of an educational system based on testing when I look out into a room full of students. After years of cramming, memorizing, regurgitating, and forgetting, many students enter college with little intellectual curiosity, much less a sense of academic excitement. Too often, the students just want to be told what they need to learn to pass the test or what they need to write to get a good grade on a paper. Because so much of their schooling has been based on this dysfunctional model, they have forgotten how to be the self-directed and genuine learners that they were when they first entered school.[3]

I recently came across an online forum where young readers were asked about the most frustrating part of high school. Reading the responses was both depressing and a damning indictment of a school system that has a detrimental impact on education. Those commenting shared horror stories, concerns, and missed opportunities—a tapestry of disappointment and conflict. Unfortunately, this isn't a problem confined to the United States. Consider this post from Rin Shimizu, a student in Malaysia, discussing a recent experience in her chemistry class:

> **Teacher:** We're gonna learn about Gibbs Free Energy today. All you need to know is this little symbol, yes,

this one here. If there is a negative sign in front of the symbol, then a reaction is spontaneous. If there is a positive sign, the reaction is not spontaneous.

Me: Why? Why's that?

Teacher: It's just the way it is. That's all you need to know.

Me: Surely there is some reason behind that? I've heard that whether a reaction is spontaneous is related to the enthalpy of a reaction...

Teacher: That's true, but all you need to know is that if there is a negative sign...

This is basically what happens in most of my classes. Questions inquiring beyond the syllabus? Slapped down! Classes are to prepare us for exams and to ace the syllabus, not to acquire knowledge for the sake of learning.[4]

Under this broken model of education, children are taught what to think—as if there exists a base set of core knowledge that every single person needs to learn to be successful in life. Children are provided with dates, names, events, processes, equations, and other information to be memorized and regurgitated—but rarely actually used. Reason and inquiry are unnecessary in a system where teachers provide information and then quiz students based on whether they remember it and not whether they actually understand it.

This is a problem.

CLINGING TO STRUCTURE

I remember owning one of those daily calendars where each day presented a different comic. Mine featured the dry-humored *Far Side* series. In one comic, a student with a small head interrupted the class to ask his teacher, "May I be excused? My brain is full." It may be humorous to suggest that information overload is a possibility, but reality tells a different story. Unlike a child's belly or bladder, the brain has an effectively limitless storage capacity. Nearly a billion neurons, each of which connects to nearly 1,000 other neurons, produce a seemingly inexhaustible web of opportunity to store memories. Brains are marvelous creations!

So the issue isn't information overload per se; we don't need to worry about our children being subjected to too many facts and figures. The question is one of *organization* and *relevance*.

From their first days, children are on a mission to make sense of the world around them. They constantly observe their surroundings, process what they see, and try to observe patterns that might predict future behavior. My children understand that when I pick up one of their books, I'm going to ask if I can read to them. If I open a bag of their favorite fruit, I'm going to offer them some. If I buckle my seat belt, I'm going to immediately ask if they've buckled theirs yet. Each task or technique they're taught—whether through observation and imitation or communication from a parent, peer, or sibling—has direct applicability to their lives. It makes sense, has context, and empowers them.

This process of natural learning is discarded in the modern education system and replaced with an arbitrary one. Parents and teachers call it "structure." I call it the slow death of curiosity.

Government schools are extremely regimented, both in logistics and learning. Rigorous schedules shuffle children from one classroom to the next, with allotted times for breaks and lunch. Teachers are given a specific amount of time to teach each group of children, and when the bell rings, the learning must immediately be stopped so that the student can go to the next period. What message does this fragmentation convey?

John Taylor Gatto thinks it conveys indifference and encourages children not to care too much about anything. Gatto was a teacher for nearly three decades in New York, being named New York State Teacher of the Year in 1991—the same year he quit teaching, penning an op-ed in The *Wall Street Journal* explaining that he was no longer willing "to hurt kids."[5] His time in the trenches led him to become an outspoken critic of what he called "prime training for permanent underclasses"[6]—a dumbing down of the general population. Of the highly structured schedules found in modern education, Gatto writes:

But when the bell rings I insist [my students] drop whatever it is we have been doing and proceed quickly to the next work station. They must turn on and off like a light switch. Nothing important is ever finished in my class or in any class I know of. Students never have a complete experience except on the installment plan.

Indeed, the lesson of bells is that no work is worth finishing, so why care too deeply about anything? Years of bells will condition all but the strongest to a world that can no longer offer important work to do. Bells are the secret logic of school time; their logic is inexorable. Bells destroy the past and future, rendering every interval the same as any other, as the abstraction of a map renders every living mountain and river the same, even though they are not. Bells inoculate each undertaking with indifference.[7]

Time is structured in school, but the content itself is even more packaged and processed before being presented to students. Curriculum committees, textbook developers, school boards, and other faceless groups of people whose motives and goals we do not know—and perhaps do not share—conspire to create lesson plans and curriculum standards that become the narrow tunnel through which all students must pass. Compulsory education being what it is, this structure is not a mere suggestion for students—it is required, under the threat of force. There are no detours available, and pausing is out of the question; students are compelled to continue crawling through the tunnel at whatever speed their masters decide.

These and other structural problems fail to account for your child's specific strengths and weaknesses, and your goals as a parent. They don't tolerate customization based on a student's interests and desires. Studying things outside the mandated structure is acceptable during the child's free time, but that's unlikely to happen; free time is assaulted by assignments from the teacher.

Interestingly, parents who enroll their children in a private school, or educate them in the home, often see structure as a coveted and necessary supplement to their child's education. Fearing having to "reinvent the wheel" or become a subject matter expert in every field of inquiry in order for their child to learn, parents naturally seek support from those who have gone before. After all, how is a mom who graduated in English or nursing supposed to know how to teach her child about algebra, physics, or world history?

The problem this presents is that parents adopt and embrace the modern education system—with all its problems—as their own. They may be "homeschooling," but they've simply reduced the size and location of their child's class. They become agents of the state within their own sanctuary, replicating the very methods they should instead be abandoning.

Put simply, highly structured schooling systems push kids through arbitrary processes that make no sense. The assignments and projects and tests often don't apply to their lives. They wonder why they need to know the dates of the Spanish Inquisition or the intricacies of photosynthesis. They are made to feel—even if they can't articulate it—like enslaved robots, following orders and becoming programmed to comport with somebody else's design. No wonder so many children rebel!

One-size-fits-all structures treat children as commodities—homogenous products to be impressed upon by the same process and system. Little if any consideration is given to the child's interests, abilities, talents, or goals. Completion of assigned tasks and getting through the material is the primary goal.

I do not want my children to be cogs in a machine, or dehumanized lemmings being led about by people who do not have their best interests at heart. My children are individuals, with talents and interests that should not be suppressed or sidelined in order to follow an educational path that somebody else deems best. Structure is often seen by parents and professional educators as a means to an end, but it has become an end unto itself.

Let me be clear: structure is not inherently evil or always unhelpful. If it is balanced out with some of the solutions we will discuss later, it can certainly have its place—and even be beneficial. But structured schooling has been considered by too many people, for far too long, as the proverbial treasure map of education: if only we follow the map's instructions, walking 50 steps ahead, then turning right and walking 30 steps, we will surely arrive at the treasure chest that awaits us. But that pot of gold is a mirage; education is not a destination—it's a process and lifestyle.

By imposing strict guidelines and requiring the memorization of useless information and the completion of arbitrary tasks, we undermine the very reason the structure supposedly exists in the first place: to introduce children to new ideas and inspire them to seek understanding. Textbooks, workbooks, syllabi, and standardized exams bury children in often meaningless and context-less busywork that on the surface appears to convey knowledge to children, but more often breeds resentment, frustration, and an increasing intolerance towards the very information they otherwise might be thrilled to learn.

This is a problem.

INDUSTRIALIZATION

Have you ever been to a factory? I marvel at the innovation and systematization you can find in factories. I enjoy showing my children videos featuring different production facilities around the world and how the products inside are assembled. These machines and processes have dramatically increased our quality of life by creating high quality products for affordable prices—from clothing to cars, and everything in-between. A simple stroll through any supermarket or retail store is a testament to the explosion of commodities that factories can produce.

Children are *not* commodities, yet the modern education system is designed to treat them as such. It's unsurprising, really. Think of it: if you were suddenly put in charge of educating millions of children, how would you do it? How *could* you? Like a factory manager, you would be focused on efficiency and an elimination of as many variables as possible. In other words, production increases as differences decrease. A shirt factory can't produce very many shirts if each one is a different size and design. But when the machine is built to produce the same design and size, it can churn them out very quickly.

That is what is being done to children in the modern education system. Just as factories are not designed to produce variety, the modern education system is not designed to produce independent thinkers. Children newly enrolled in a government school, for example, take an initial step onto a conveyor belt. All children produce the same work and take the same tests. They are conditioned to learn and repeat the same information. If they act as expected, they are rewarded, given approval, and allowed to continue along the conveyor belt. Those who resist are reprimanded and branded as inadequate. From there, they continue to be poked, prodded, twisted, molded, packaged, and served up as a final result—a "graduate" with a "degree" testifying to the fact that they stayed on the conveyor belt from beginning to end.

Part of the problem with industrialization is the classification of education as a product, rather than a service. When I go to the store, I can select from off-the-shelf products that have been made available for purchase. I can't change what is offered; the manufacturer has mass produced what is now in front of me. I can take it or leave it. Contrast that experience with getting a haircut, where the stylist is extremely attentive to your needs and desires. If you want your hair shampooed or colored, that can be done. When one side is looking a little shorter than the other, the stylist can address the issue and follow your instructions. You control the experience, within limits, and have a wide range of outcomes from which to choose. That's because a haircut is a service. Like having your car worked on, a website created, or your landscape maintained, you are appreciated and served; your interests are the focus of attention at all times.

Unfortunately, the modern education system has become so centralized and commoditized that education is largely perceived as a product; the interests of the end consumer are secondary at best. One need only ask for an exception from a school's standardized curriculum to see how the features of a service—deference to the preference of the individual—are unlikely to be found within the walls of today's schools. The mass production manufacturing model has been applied to education, bringing all of the processes found in factories: top-down controls, strict standards, chains of command, rule enforcement, and widespread data collection. We wouldn't hire a service provider who refused to do what we asked of them. Why, then, do we tolerate this inflexible, industrialized approach when it comes to our children?

While this is not a history book, it's important to understand that the industrialization of education is not mere happenstance—it is intentional and by design. The modern education system began nearly two centuries ago, when reformers and politicians in America sought to adopt the system used in Prussia. This method, which was quite different from how children had been educated for millennia, focused on career training and standardized information through a regulated curriculum for each grade and widespread testing to ensure that children were adequately performing as they proceeded through the system. Prussia was one of the first countries to compel school attendance and pay for it through taxation. In addition to testing and top-down standards, their education system provided for teacher training and mandatory kindergarten.

Horace Mann, one of the leading education reformers in America in the mid-19th century, admired the system being developed in Prussia, and the results it appeared to produce. Following a trip abroad to see it in action for himself, he became a strong advocate for its implementation in America.

This lobbying effort was swift and successful. Mann was instrumental in getting Massachusetts to adopt the Prussian model of education statewide in 1852, and other states soon followed. What emerged in the years ahead was a new kind of school called—I kid you not—the "factory model school," where both the design of the school building and the processes used within it were modeled after an actual factory. The rest, as we know, is history—and the present reality for millions of children who are at various stages of their own conveyor belt experience.

Again, ask yourself: how would you do it differently if you were in charge of the education system for the entire nation? Or, bite off a smaller chunk: what would you do to educate the tens of thousands of children in a single community? As one high school principal put it, "When you get 150 students who need to pass their exams to move on, all you're worried about is efficiency, and the score on the test at the end of the semester."[8] Secondary interests fall by the wayside as the conveyor belt marches onward. Factories only survive when they are efficient.

An increasingly worse development was on the horizon in the form of John Dewey and his associates who arrived on the scene a few decades later. Mann's quest to industrialize education set up a framework that other education reformers were then able to use to indoctrinate millions of children. It's not a surprise, is it? The factories were set up, and that automation and structure became a tool for others to use for nefarious ends.

John Dewey was a secular humanist whose atheist utopia required controlling the masses by shaping the minds of the rising generation. His book, *My Pedagogic Creed*, demonstrates the thinking behind his significant influence on education in America at the opening of the twentieth century: "I believe that every teacher should realize the dignity of his calling; that he is a social servant set apart for the maintenance of proper social order and the securing of the right social growth. I believe that in this way the teacher always is the prophet of the true God and the usherer in of the true kingdom of God."[9] Dewey's "true God" and "true kingdom" were government.

Over a century ago, the industrialization of education enabled Dewey and his like-minded cohorts to "build up forces... whose natural effect is to undermine the importance and uniqueness of family life."[10] Academics were secondary; social transformation was the key, and families stood in the way. The "importance of public schools" facilitated, for Dewey and his allies, "the relaxation of older family ties."[11] The intent, fundamentally, was to weaken a child's family relationships and strengthen his or her relationship to—and dependence upon—the state. As one prominent official in the National Education Association said in 1934, "The major function of the school is the social orientation of the individual. It must seek to give him understanding of the transition to a new social order."[12] Is that really why parents send their children to school? It may not be their desire, but it certainly can be one of the consequences.

All of this may sound odd. You may feel, like most parents, that the average school teacher is a well-intentioned individual simply trying to help children learn—and I agree. But a tiny and dispensable component, as part of a much larger machine, neither understands nor is able to significantly impact the overall complexity and purpose of that machine. The modern education system was set up to condition children and produce results favorable to the individuals involved in overseeing it. They don't have an individual child's best interest in mind, nor can they tolerate his or her unique interests and abilities. Like any factory manager, they have to reduce variables and streamline processes in order to ensure a consistent, predictable output.

Critics of the industrialization of food contend that the products you and I buy at the grocery store lack both flavor and nutrition. Genetic manipulation has allowed for brighter colors and longer shelf life, so that shoppers are impressed and store owners can maximize profits. But these characteristics come at a sacrifice, because the actual qualities of the food decline while emphasis is placed on the superficial qualities. The same can be said of modern schools that focus on superficialities rather than substance. Obedience, attendance, memorization, and regurgitation are the primary metrics of modern schools and give the appearance of an education, but do not guarantee your child is actually learning and improving.

This is a problem.

AUTHORITARIANISM

A popular, though fake, image continues to spread through social media depicting a teacher's letter informing a mother that her insubordinate child Alex was sentenced to detention. What did this fictional Alex do that was wrong? "He consistently defied me," wrote the pretend teacher. "During class he contradicted me numerous times when I insisted that the length of one kilometer was greater than that of one mile."

It gets more interesting. The letter continued: "Although he was correct, Alex's actions show a blatant disregard for authority, and a complete lack of respect for his school. In the future, Alex would be better off simply accepting my teachings without resistance." While it was not a real letter, online forums are filled with people posting their own similar—and real—experiences facing authoritarian teachers.

One person recalled how his English teacher deducted points from a paper he wrote, circling "for all intents and purposes" and writing "for all *intensive* purposes" as a "correction." Twenty minutes of class debate ensued after the student challenged the teacher, who would neither relent nor change his grade. Another child's teacher insisted, incorrectly, that pineapples grow on trees. When the eight-year-old student pointed out that they grew on the ground—a fact he knew from personal observation on a trip to Puerto Rico—she was disciplined and accused of arrogance. A third commenter corrected his teacher who had stated that a person's behavior was determined by the phases of the moon, reasoning that just as tides are affected by the moon, so too are our bodies, which are mostly comprised of water. The student's desk was turned backwards and pushed to the back of the classroom, where he was required to sit for the remainder of the school year. His parents were informed that he had "disrupted" the class.[13]

This tradition of placing more emphasis on authority than actual truth is troubling. Parents and teachers should be facilitators of children acquiring knowledge. Unfortunately, too often, they are perceived to be the source. It gets worse when that supposed source is distanced and abstracted—when central planners who lack a connection to or interest in the needs of individual children produce the information that students are required to learn. These planners may come in the form of politicians and curriculum committees who dictate standards, or textbook manufacturers who create books to teach those standards. Are these individuals vetted? How can we identify their biases and philosophies? Why should we take them at their words and treat their statements as unquestionable facts?

While many people in the modern education system are authoritarian, so, too, is the process itself. This top-down approach to centrally planning the education of the entire rising generation demonstrates, to quote a college professor, "the desire to engineer the learning experiences of every child."[14] There are many education problems to solve, the professor acknowledges, "but one-size-fits-all modeling, accompanied by the seemingly limitless urge to repackage and sell old ideas as new ones" produces a constant stream of "education reforms" from government at all levels. He continues:

> States adopt untested teacher evaluation frameworks whole-hog, and the federal government

attaches new strings to desperately needed federal funding without investigating the effectiveness of its preferred approaches first. In each case, the solution comes before the problem is properly defined, and it comes with a dictum that cannot be ignored. This is the solution, we're told. Now go implement it.[15]

Education should be about inquiry and investigation—an open-minded review of information as it is discovered and dissected. Ideas should rise and fall on their merits, and we should constantly be adapting and progressing, ever trying to find the best ways to do things. But this cannot happen when you have the few deciding for the many. Unaccountable and fallible "deciders" who plan the educational roadmap of over a decade of a child's life end up making completely arbitrary decisions about what information children should be exposed to, and tested on.

These educrats, as I like to call them, perpetually produce programs that continue to fail, leading to one iteration after another. The No Child Left Behind Act, Race to the Top, the Common Core State Standards Initiative, the Every Student Succeeds Act, and a host of other "reforms" are the hallmarks of the federal government's failure in education, and a natural consequence of authoritarianism in education. And while many feel that "local control" in education would be superior, it still relies on authority and involves the few deciding the education of the many—albeit *fewer* "few" and *fewer* "many" than at a national level. This approach is not inherently better simply because the decision makers live down the street, rather than in another state.

Every parent should be concerned about the nature and effects of authoritarianism when it comes to the education of their child. At best, the child ends up developing an unhealthy dependence upon authority figures rather than acquiring knowledge and formulating an opinion. Deference to authority permeates our society and has led to a submissive, ignorant culture that bases opinion on what a few information brokers—elected officials, news reporters, etc.—tell us about what we should worry. At worst, however, authoritarianism leads undeveloped minds to unquestioningly embrace propaganda as truth. There's a reason why all of the most ruthless governments throughout world history made so much effort to control the education of the youth: children are easily molded to believe what they are told, and those who control the opinions of the rising generation control the future. Political theorist Hannah Arendt once noted that the goal of truly authoritarian education "has never been to instill conviction but to destroy the capacity to form any."[16] Top-down controllers want pliable people—not resistance and unregulated diversity of thought and action. This is why Adolf Hitler once said, "He alone who owns the youth, gains the future."[17] He believed it, and acted accordingly. Shouldn't we?

The reality of world history cannot be ignored, and the widespread (and catastrophic) effects of authoritarian education methodologies must be heeded by every concerned parent. Conditioning children to look to their teacher or textbook as the source of unquestionable truth breeds an unhealthy dependence that will be difficult to overcome as an adult. It also sets children up to become controlled by others. If your child is on a factory conveyor belt, then he is subject to the whim and will of whomever controls the machine, and a conveyor belt that mass produces subservient citizens is a very enticing system that tempts a wide range of people, from well-intentioned (though misguided) education reformers to power-hungry utopian tyrants hoping to shape society into their ideal image.

This is a problem.

AGE SEGREGATION

Imagine yourself as a 50-year-old empty nester. Suddenly you have a significant increase in free time as the children are off leading their lives. Things are quiet at home, and you decide to enroll in some classes at the local university to sharpen your skills or learn about an issue that has always intrigued you. Walking into your class for the first time, you immediately observe that the other students appear to be similar to you. You ask around and confirm that everybody else is a 50-year-old empty nester, too.

The situation runs counter to what you might expect, namely, that your classmates would be diverse in age and background—mostly young adult college students, with perhaps a few older folks sprinkled in. It seems unnatural to be confined to a class where the primary characteristic shared in common among all the students is the span of months in which they emerged from their mothers' wombs. For you, as an adult, this arrangement would be weird. For children, however, age segregation can be detrimental.

The effects of age segregation include not only a loss of healthy and diverse relationships, but a generational breakdown. Nancy Henin runs Temple University's Intergenerational Center and notes, "If you have institutions that are focused on different age groups," the result can be "negative stereotypes and people feeling isolated from each other."[18] This ageism pits groups against each other; teenagers perceive senior citizens to be weak and worthless, while the elderly dismiss the rising generation as a bunch of mischievous hooligans. Segregation breeds division and competition, whereas most parents likely want their children to learn collaboration and community.

To some degree, grouping students by age makes sense. Many people often prefer to associate with their peers who share similar cultural preferences, educational backgrounds, or life experience. College students want to party late into the night with others who wish to do the same, whereas the elderly prefer peace and quiet, and want to be surrounded by those who also go to bed early. This voluntary self-selection is, however, at odds with the compulsory separation by school administrators who believe, apparently, that those of like age should learn the same things in the same way. This model—again, a recent experiment in human history—has been strongly criticized since its inception, though never abolished. Consider this rebuke, written by a university president:

> The class system has been modeled upon the military system. It is constructed upon the assumption that a group of minds can be marshaled and controlled in growth in exactly the same manner that a military officer marshals and directs the bodily movements of a company of soldiers. In solid, unbreakable phalanx the class is supposed to move through all the grades, keeping in locked step. This locked step is set by the 'average' pupil—an algebraic myth born of inanimate figures and an addled pedagogy.
>
> The class system does permanent violence to all types of pupils. It does injury to the rapid and quick-thinking pupils, because these must shackle their stride to keep pace with the mythical average… The class system does a greater injury to the large number who make slower progress than the rate of the

mythical average pupil. Necessarily they are carried off their feet by the momentum of the mass. They are foredoomed to failure before they begin.[19]

That was written in 1913.

The author, Frederic Burk, was the first president of a teacher-training college that became California State University at San Francisco. Burk saw over a century ago the problem that persists to this day—that educating children in batches, according to their age, is unnatural and harmful to the individuality of each child. Following his rebuke, Burk asked, "Could any system be more stupid in its assumptions, more impossible in its conditions, and more juggernautic in its operation?" And yet, despite objections and reform proposals, the age segregation system continues undeterred.

One might expect a child's educational experience to gradually introduce them to the real world by incorporating ideas, systems, and relationships that they will increasingly rely on as they mature. And yet, age segregation creates a fake world for children, requiring them to interact primarily, and sometimes exclusively, with people of their same age. At what point in your adult life have you associated with a group of people based on their age alone? It doesn't happen. Why, then, would we subject our children to this?

In an ideal world, schools might model themselves after the home environment—the primary and natural setting in which children learn and thrive. But as noted earlier, the architects of the modern education system wanted to substitute that ideal world for their own utopian scheme. They aimed to substitute the state for the role and rule of family government. In other words, they wanted to put an arbitrary school system in place of the natural family system, in order to impose their designs upon the masses.

Those designs include separating children from the diverse relationships they otherwise might form with people of differing backgrounds, ages, and abilities. Whereas families and communities naturally include such diversity, which allows youth to learn from and model their elders and provides older children with an opportunity to nurture and lead the young, the age segregation found in schools removes these natural relationships, emphasizing the importance and authority of the teacher. Nothing can be allowed to compete against "the prophet of the true God" in a Dewey-esque education system. While families should be served by schools, it turns out that they quickly become subordinate to them.

This is a problem.

YES, THIS APPLIES TO YOU

Okay, deep breath. Those are some profound problems to ponder. If this is all news to you, at this point you're probably either feeling like this is too much to handle or that it doesn't apply to you. Both points are wrong. Allow me to explain why.

We live in a world of influencers; our opinions are constantly shaped by external forces encouraging us to buy a new product, try a new service, or believe a certain idea. We are bombarded with information and must constantly sift through it to determine what we want to do. Your child needs to be prepared for this world—equipped with ideas, understanding, and behavior that will empower him or her to chart a safe course through the stormy seas.

Sounds reasonable, right? To the average person, this is called "public relations"—creating messaging that will alter your behavior in a way that is desirable to those who are producing the message. Companies throughout the world do it, as do humanitarian organizations, churches, and schools. It's commonplace. But the father of public relations—the guy who quite literally "wrote the book" on the subject—didn't call it by this name. He called it by its actual name, propaganda—and titled his book *Propaganda* accordingly. His name was Edward Bernays, and his success in secretly influencing the behavior of millions of people is well established.

Bernays wrote that people "are rarely aware of the real reasons which motivate their actions," boldly explaining in great detail how people's lives can be controlled, and why he thought that "the conscious and intelligent manipulation of the organized habits and opinions of the masses is an important element in democratic society."[20] He continued:

> Those who manipulate this unseen mechanism of society constitute an invisible government which is the true ruling power of our country...

> In almost every act of our daily lives, whether in the sphere of politics or business, in our social conduct or our ethical thinking, we are dominated by the relatively small number of persons... who understand the mental processes and social patterns of the masses. It is they who pull the wires which control the public mind.[21]

It may be convenient to deny that this process still takes place and move on in our lives with decisive ignorance, but a frank assessment of how modern media works cannot lead to any other conclusion. Those who want to manufacture fear, or consumerism, or distrust, or ignorance, have the means to do so—and an ample track record of their tragic success. So while we, as adults, must take care not to be manipulated ourselves, it is into this world that our precious children are being introduced. As parents we are not only nurturers, but protectors—and we must take active steps to appropriately shield them from both the evil intentions of would-be tyrants and the well-intentioned, though misguided, designs of central planners. In few ways are our children so profoundly affected as in their education—literally, the way their opinions and beliefs are shaped.

This is not too much to handle. It's what we, as parents, do.

And that leads to my second point: this most definitely applies to you. If you're a parent of a child in public or charter school, it is imperative to understand the problems in that system so you can try to counteract them in the home. Private schools, while not funded by taxpayers, regularly feature the same structure, authoritarianism, and conveyor belt processes. Any parent who outsources the education of their child to another individual or institution must be aware of the concerns that arrangement necessarily raises—and the issues outlined in this chapter are extremely applicable to these institutions.

Or, perhaps you homeschool your child, having recognized some of these problems and opted out of the group schooling paradigm. If so, you may have read this chapter while patting yourself on the back, thinking that your family's decision has spared your child from what's been discussed. While this may be true in part, many homeschool families do not correct these concerns. Instead, they replicate them, believing that homeschool means incorporating school into the home—as if a geographical change itself will allow them to steer clear of these problems.

In other words, many homeschooling families are heavily reliant upon structured curriculum and conveyor belt methodologies, albeit slightly more customizable ones. Parents turn themselves into teachers and feel that the very small class size compensates for the deficiencies of the modern education system, likely not realizing the many other problems they are recreating and, therefore, validating.

What's been written here could be expanded to fill volumes, especially by analyzing the people who have brought us to this point, their motives, and their philosophies; we are a byproduct, in many ways, of those who have gone before us. Suffice it to say that the modern education system, as it's commonly implemented and understood, is an absolute disaster.

ENDNOTES

1. H.L. Mencken, "The Little Red Schoolhouse," *The American Mercury, vol. 1*, (New York: Alfred Knoff, 1924) 504.
2. "When Memorization Gets in the Way of Learning," *The Atlantic*, September 9, 2013, http://www.theatlantic.com/education/archive/2013/09/when-memorization-gets-in-the-way-of-learning/279425/.
3. "Cram. Memorize. Regurgitate. Forget.," *Everyday Sociology Blog*, April 26, 2012, http://www.everyday-sociologyblog.com/2012/04/cram-memorize-regurgitate-forget.html.
4. "What is the most frustrating thing about being a high school student?," *Quora*, https://www.quora.com/What-is-the-most-frustrating-thing-about-being-a-high-school-student.
5. "I Quit, I Think," *The Wall Street Journal*, July 25, 1991.
6. John Taylor Gatto, *Dumbing Us Down: The Hidden Curriculum of Compulsory Schooling* (Gabriola Island: New Society Publishers, 2005), 16.
7. Ibid., 6.
8. Kelsey Leigh Stokes, "The Impact of the Factory Model of Education in Central Texas," Baylor University Thesis, November 2013.
9. Jo Ann Boydston, ed., *The Early Works of John Dewey, vol 5* (Carbondale: Southern Illinois University Press, 2008), 95.

10. Jo Ann Boydston, ed., *The Later Works of John Dewey, vol. 3* (Carbondale: Southern Illinois University Press, 2008), 230.
11. Ibid., 409.
12. "The Public School Curriculum," *A. A. S. A. Official Report, Including a Record of the Annual Convention*, 1934.
13. "The Curious Case of Adam Hilliker," *1chance2learn. net*, August 29, 2012, http://1chance2learn.blogspot.com/2012/08/the-curious-case-of-adam-hilliker.html.
14. "The tyranny of top-down education reform," *The Washington Post*, July 21, 2015, https://www.washingtonpost.com/news/answer-sheet/wp/2015/07/21/the-tyranny-of-top-down-education-reform-or-if-everyone-has-school-choice-is-it-still-a-choice/.
15. Ibid.
16. Hannah Arendt, *Totalitarianism* (New York: Harcourt Brace Jovanovic, 1968), 168.
17. Jennifer Keeley, *Life in the Hitler Youth* (San Diego: Lucent Books, 1999), 8–10.
18. "What 'age segregation' does to America," *The Boston Globe*, August 31, 2014.
19. Frederic Burk, *Lock-step Schooling and a Remedy* (Sacramento: F.W. Richardson, 1913), 7.
20. Edward Bernays, *Propaganda* (New York: IG Publishing, 1928), 37.
21. Ibid.

"Education has for its object the formation of character. To curb restive propensities, to awaken dormant sentiments, to strengthen the perceptions, and cultivate the tastes, to encourage this feeling and repress that, so as finally to develop the child into a man of well-proportioned and harmonious nature—this is alike the aim of parent and teacher."[1]

—HERBERT SPENCER

———∽∞∾———

TWO

WHAT ARE YOUR GOALS?

On June 25, 2010, 18-year-old Erica Goldson stood at a podium in front of her peers and their parents. Behind her sat the administrators and teachers of the school from which she was graduating. As school valedictorian, Erica now had the opportunity to speak to her graduating class.

To say that Erica's words were unexpected would be a tremendous understatement. The speech was akin to dropping a grenade into a foxhole filled with both wounded warriors and war generals. It rebuked the very institution in which she excelled and condemned the life work of the salaried school staff who supported her. But where many took offense, others received inspiration from the accurate and honest assessment of the problems through which Erica and her peers had navigated.

"I cannot say that I am any more intelligent than my peers," Erica said. "I can attest that I am only the best at doing what I am told and working the system." She continued:

> Yet, here I stand, and I am supposed to be proud that I have completed this period of indoctrination. I will leave in the fall to go on to the next phase expected of me, in order to receive a paper document that certifies that I am capable of work. But I contest that I am a human being, a thinker, an adventurer—not a worker. A worker is someone who is trapped within repetition—a slave of the system set up before him. But now, I have successfully shown that I was the best slave. I did what I was told to the extreme.[2]

Ouch.

If the modern education system is a conveyor belt of manufactured learning, then Erica was the Grade A product—the very best commodity the system had produced. She was superior to the rest, jumping through every hoop and following the system's guidelines to the letter. But at what cost? Erica explains:

> While others sat in class and doodled to later become great artists, I sat in class to take notes and become a great test-taker.
>
> While others would come to class without their homework done because they were reading about an interest of theirs, I never missed an assignment.

While others were creating music and writing lyrics, I decided to do extra credit, even though I never needed it.

So, I wonder, why did I even want this position? Sure, I earned it, but what will come of it? When I leave educational institutionalism, will I be successful or forever lost? I have no clue about what I want to do with my life; I have no interests because I saw every subject of study as work, and I excelled at every subject just for the purpose of excelling, not learning. And quite frankly, now I'm scared.[3]

If a model student like Erica is terrified of her future, and ill-equipped to face it, then what is the point of the system at all? The quality of output compels us to question the process used to create it. Having addressed some of the problems in the modern education system, we must now consider the question of what, exactly, we want for our children. Do we want them to become expert test takers and instruction followers? Or, perhaps, should they strive to be something more than a human equivalent of Pavlov's dog?

WHAT'S THE IDEAL OUTPUT?

What do you want for your child? This fundamental question should lie at the foundation of our approach to education, and yet few parents ponder it to any significant degree. They largely let others do the thinking for them and assume that enrolling the child in a certain school, or requiring them to pass through certain curricula, will result in a praiseworthy output.

But children are neither cogs in a machine nor raw goods waiting to be processed into homogeneous products. Yet this is how the system is designed. Today's standardized school system focuses on making children "college and career ready," prioritizing above all else a continuation of the conveyor belt until adulthood arrives. Even then, the results have been dismal; a survey of 165,000 high school students in 2015 found that only 45% of them felt positive about their college and career readiness.[4]

I consider "college and career ready" a pretty pathetic barometer of a child's success in acquiring knowledge—as if the value of 13 years of education were determined by whether the graduate recalls enough information to pass an entrance exam or has a GPA high enough to please a potential employer. There's much more to life than this.

Further, college and careers should be viewed with the proper perspective: they are means to an end, rather than the ends themselves. Learning and working enable us to provide for our families, become productive members of society, create products or services that benefit others, and pursue other interests outside of work. Nearly a decade and a half of education should be enough of a setup to prepare children for a meaningful future and to help them develop a quality of character that will enrich their lives.

The things I want for my children can't be assessed by a test or learned in a workbook. I want them to develop vibrant personalities and qualities such as courage, leadership, creativity, empathy, persistence, innovation, resilience, motivation, etc. I want them to be constantly curious and eager to use their talents in the service of others. These, and a host of other positive traits, are what any parent wants for their children. But can we rely on problem-ridden education methodologies to cultivate them?

More than anything, we want our children to be prepared for their future—equipped with the tools and training necessary to navigate their way through uncharted territory. That preparation won't come by regurgitation or standardized examination. In short, schools do not provide your child with what he or she needs. A different process—a different path—is needed.

Part of the challenge for parents is that a child's path is not linear and safely guarded by padded rails on either side. Given the unpredictability of the future, it's better to visualize each person's life as having a large number of forks in the road, presenting choices, and corresponding consequences, depending on which direction the child chooses to travel. Rapid changes in technology are making many professions obsolete and creating entirely new ones; attending school to learn a skill is no guarantee that that skill will be in demand for years to come. Consider today's managers of e-commerce companies, many of whom went to college before the industry even existed. It's better to anticipate uncertainty and develop skills that have general application—leadership, ingenuity, curiosity, persistence, etc.—than to put all your educational eggs in one career basket. We want our children to be successful no matter how the economy changes or what circumstances they face as they go through life.

A few months after the valedictorian speech, Erica was asked to suggest three pieces of advice she would give to high school freshmen, who themselves are stepping into an unpredictable world. She offered the following:

> 1. Don't take school too seriously. Sometimes that picture you're drawing is more important than studying for your Spanish test.

> 2. Get involved. Find your passions and explore them even more by joining or forming clubs.

> 3. Meet a lot of people. Learn as much as you can about what other people think and how little you actually know.[5]

You'll notice that she didn't emphasize getting good grades, doing all your homework, or making sure to thoroughly complete the curriculum. Instead, her sound advice, if implemented, will lead a child to new experiences, new relationships, new perspectives, and an enriched sense of community and personal character—all things that parents desire in a well-rounded child primed for success in life. After all, the best lessons in life are often not found in a book.

CRITICAL THINKING

Perhaps one of the most important goals parents should establish for their children—and one of the characteristics that the modern education system utterly fails to cultivate—is that of critical thinking: the ability to objectively evaluate an issue to form a judgment. Put differently, critical thinking involves questioning proposed information, formulating arguments for or against it, and making decisions based on presented evidence.

Critical thinking is inherently anti-authoritarian. Those who have this capacity do not accept information merely because of its source. "Because I said so" isn't good enough; ideas must rise and fall based on the message, rather than the messenger.

Later, I will present you with several successful education models that abandon authoritarianism in favor of developing a debate and discussion of ideas. Many in the "mainstream" educational establishment struggle with these approaches, because critical thinking is difficult to quantify, and therefore difficult to assess. In other words, school administrators can't sit your child down, give them a fill-in-the-bubble exam, and compute a score to see if he or she has developed this trait.

The educational models we'll explore in the pages ahead are branded as "alternative" merely because they are not "mainstream." But this is actually backwards; the assessment-driven, authority-based school systems of the past century are a recent development in human history, whereas student-centric approaches have long existed. For example, the Socratic method—where learners are engaged in an analytic discussion, rather than a passive presentation—is over 2,400 years old. Reformers like to be "new" and "fresh," with an ever-changing criteria of "best practices," but the results of lecture-based learning are consistently poor. For example, a 2005 study showed that only 15 percent of high school seniors who were already deemed "proficient" in writing were actually able to write well-organized essays in which they took clear positions and consistently supported those positions with evidence. Even worse, only six percent of them could make informed, critical judgments about written text they were asked to read.[6]

The risk is clear: those who cannot formulate coherent arguments and analyze supporting statements are susceptible to believing falsehoods. An ignorant society is a gullible society, easily led down dangerous paths based on misinformation, propaganda, and fear of the unknown. Critical thinking, on the other hand, empowers a person to discern facts from spin and arrive at conclusions and decisions that are evidenced-based and supportable by reason and objective data.

Another issue is that educational reformers have turned critical thinking into a buzzword that lacks any real meaning. Common Core—one of the more controversial sets of school standards in recent history— describes itself as "developing the critical-thinking, problem-solving, and analytical skills students will need to be successful."[7] Yet, these standards were not tested, provided no evidence of their ability to meet these claims, and were forced onto millions of children throughout the United States of America—children who were effectively turned into human guinea pigs as part of a massive experiment in education. Thus we see that the very arguments used to convince legislators to implement Common Core discouraged dissent; and once put in place, the assessment methods the program used could not measure the creativity, experimentation, and debate that critical thinking requires.

Critical thinking is a term that has been co-opted, much like a snake oil salesman's use of the word "cure" to describe his worthless product. The simple fact that the term has been increasingly bandied about does not mean that more people are actually developing the skills and techniques that equate to critical thinking. As of 2014, "mentions of critical thinking in job postings ha[d] doubled since 2009," according to *The Wall Street Journal*. Their analysis found that "more than 21,000 health-care and 6,700 management postings contained some reference to the skill." Yet, despite the desire of employers to find would-be workers with the trait, "bosses stumble when pressed to describe exactly what skills make critical thinkers."[8] Let that sink in—even those looking for employees who possess critical thinking skills cannot define what critical thinking skills are. The words have entirely lost their meaning.

Parents who want their children to become independent-minded adults, able to differentiate between sound and faulty reasoning, must make sure that critical thinking does not remain a mere buzzword. It is a necessary character trait—a persistent desire to question, analyze, and seek new perspectives and learning.

It's also important to recognize that critical thinking does not exist in a vacuum. Rather, it is a layer built on top of a foundation of basic knowledge. Children won't become subject matter experts merely by questioning and critiquing everything they're told. In many subjects, and especially at the introductory levels of each subject, there are fundamental and well-established rules and truths that simply need to be learned. Before your children become thinkers, they must first be learners; we cannot evaluate what we do not understand.

The role of the teacher is transformed under the critical thinking model. Unlike the authoritarian approach where teachers provide both the questions and answers, while the student's job is to listen and sometimes ask a question of their own, the critical thinking model requires students to provide both the questions and the answers, while the teachers merely facilitate and guide discussion. This shift encourages self-directed, independent learning, enabling children to take ownership of their education—a necessary aspect of passion-driven education, which we'll explore later.

I emphasize the importance of critical thinking, as we ponder what our parental goals are, because of its enduring relevance—and, sadly, its short supply in our society. Its primary benefit, for both individuals and society at large, was eloquently articulated by William Sumner, the first professor of sociology in America:

> The critical habit of thought, if usual in society, will pervade all its mores, because it is a way of taking up the problems of life. Men educated in it cannot be stampeded by stump orators and are never deceived by dithyrambic [wildly enthusiastic] orators. They are slow to believe. They can hold things as possible or probable in all degrees, without certainty and

without pain. They can wait for evidence and weigh evidence, uninfluenced by the emphasis or confidence with which assertions are made on one side or the other. They can resist appeals to their dearest prejudices and all kinds of cajolery. Education in the critical faculty is the only education of which it can be truly said that it makes good citizens.[9]

Our challenge as parents is that we cannot predict what life will be like for our children. There is no set of formulas or facts we can drill into them that will be guaranteed to help them resolve a future marital conflict, workplace challenge, legal battle, or any number of other circumstances in which they may find themselves. The modern education system might have you think otherwise, but life is not merely about acquiring the maximum amount of knowledge; success for your child will not come by being able to regurgitate data. What our children need are the tools necessary to solve whatever problems they encounter.

CHARACTER DEVELOPMENT

What's more important: what your children know, or who they are?

Schools primarily focus on the former. While knowledge is important, it is becoming increasingly clear that greater attention needs to be paid to the latter. And while most concerned parents rightly focus on character development in the home, the overwhelming majority of children spend most of their day in an environment that not only fails to inspire and encourage positive character traits, but actively undermines them. It's hard to raise a virtuous leader in such a setting.

As I was researching this section of the book, I googled things like "school environment drugs profanity sex cheating" in order to find news articles, opinions, and research studies on the subject. And while some serious digging did reveal what I was looking for, almost all of the search results were policies and handbooks produced by public schools. Each of these had disciplinary guidelines established in an effort to minimize these and other problems that run rampant through large groups of children. And yet, despite good intentions and established guidelines, these problems persist.

Here's the tragic overview of the character of children today. In a confidential survey of 12,000 high school students in 2002, 74% of them admitted to having cheated on a test at least once in the past year.[10] In a 2013 study about sexual activity among adolescents, nearly half (47%) of high school students admitted to having sexual intercourse; 13% of females and 17% of males had already had more than four sexual partners in their short lives.[11] And keep in mind, these statistics only track intercourse and do not include non-intercourse sexual activity. A related and new development among 13% of 14 to 24 year olds is "sexting"—sharing naked photos or video of oneself via a mobile device.[12] Substance abuse is also quite prevalent: 23.5% of 10th graders and 37.4% of 12th graders reported past-month use of alcohol; 27.2% of high school students reported past-year use of illicit drugs; and all forms of tobacco use (*e.g.* cigarettes, hookah, e-cigarettes) remain popular.[13] Just as standardized tests can't help us track positive traits, these statistics don't report the many negative traits that are found in abundance in adolescents today: vulgarity, disrespect, carelessness, mediocrity, rebellion, bullying, etc.

In the name of academics, we have confined children to a small room with people their age, limiting their exposure to mature teens and adults who could act as mentors, positive role models, and examples of good behavior to help them become better people. Schools have become like bacteria-ridden petri dishes, waiting to corrupt any pure specimen placed inside.

As we think about the character development of our children, we need to not only give attention to the negative, but also the neutral. It's easy to observe problematic behaviors, but even "clean cut" students are often bored, apathetic, or unchallenged. Movies like *Ferris Bueller's Day Off*, with its classroom scenes of disengaged and sighing students, epitomize epitomize the essence of what many students feel while being confined to a classroom. Research published in the *Journal of Educational Psychology* in 2010 warns about the obvious dangers associated with boredom in the learning process. The study's authors found that boredom is "experienced quite frequently" in school and that "students reported that they became bored when they perceived a particular task as having little or no value to them"[14]—a finding that itself validates the very premise of passion-driven education. They continued:

> The evidence in our studies suggests that boredom typically impairs attention, motivation, behavioral strategies, and performance in achievement settings. The pervasiveness of the boredom experienced by many students, coupled with its deleterious effects, clearly implies that educators, administrators, and policy makers responsible for the design of academic settings should pay more attention to this emotion.[15]

The researchers suggest that educators "focus on increasing the perceived value of activities in achievement settings"—in other words, help children understand the importance of what they are being taught. This will be difficult when the content is forced upon them, but becomes natural and easy when using their passions to guide instruction. Bored students represent missed opportunities to inspire a rising generation to fulfill their maximum potential and become innovators and leaders in the future. They should be provided an educational environment in which they can find fulfillment and thrive. Passion-driven education, as we'll soon see, accomplishes that.

While China is often cited as a model worthy of emulation among many academic reformers of our day, it actually presents a warning. While the nation's students test at the highest levels for reading, science, and math, this alleged academic achievement comes at a cost. The country "has no problem producing mid-level accountants, computer programmers and technocrats," observes Jiang Xueqin, the deputy principal of a high school in Beijing, China. "But what about the entrepreneurs and innovators needed to run a 21st century global economy? China's most promising students still must go abroad to develop their managerial drive and creativity, and there they have to unlearn the test-centric approach to knowledge that was drilled into them." Xueqin continues by noting that the "rote-memorization system" that has become mainstream produces a "lack of social and practical skills, absence of self-discipline and imagination, loss of curiosity and passion for learning."[16] If some of the most important skills in one's life are not developed after nearly two decades of institutionalized schooling, then what was the point?

One of the U.S. Department of Education's stated goals is to "promote strong character," and congressional mandates such as the 1994 Partnerships in Character Education Program have attempted to see character development introduced in schools around the country. These efforts are set up to fail: you can't promote respect in an environment that disrespects the preferences of the individual; you can't teach justice in an unjust system that homogenizes children and ignores their basic humanity; and you can't teach personal responsibility in a world of mandates and micromanagement. Character development requires honoring the individuality of the student and allowing them to fully and freely interact with the world around them.

Erica Goldson became valedictorian—the "best slave" in a system that disregards a child's interests, abilities, and goals. Let us not abandon these higher goals in favor of the baser goals set by bureaucrats. Instead, let's embrace an educational format that has a much higher chance of turning a parent's hope for their child into a reality.

ENDNOTES

1. Herbert Spencer, *Social Statics* (New York: D. Appleton & Co., 1873), 201.
2. "Here I Stand," *America Via Erica*, June 25, 2010, http://americaviaerica.blogspot.com/p/speech.html.
3. Ibid.
4. Leal, Fermin. "Survey: Most High School Students Feel Unprepared for College, Careers." *Highlighting Strategies for Student Success*. EdSource, 30 July 2015, http://edsource.org/2015/survey-most-high-school-students-feel-unprepared-for-college-careers/83752.
5. "Why conventional education is failing us – Interview with valedictorian Erica Goldson," *The Uncommon Life*, November 15, 2010, http://www.theuncommonlife.com/blog/conventional-education-failing-us-interview-erica-goldson/.
6. Cited in George E. Newell, David Bloome, Alan Hirvela, *Teaching and Learning Argumentative Writing in High School English Language Arts Classrooms* (New York: Routledge, 2015), 4.
7. "What Parents Should Know," Common Core State Standards Initiative, http://www.corestandards.org/what-parents-should-know/.
8. "Bosses Seek 'Critical Thinking,' but What Is That?," *The Wall Street Journal*, October 21, 2014, http://www.wsj.com/articles/bosses-seek-critical-thinking-but-what-is-that-1413923730.
9. William Graham Sumner, *Folkways* (Boston: Ginn & Co., 1906), 633.

10. "A Cheating Crisis in America's Schools," ABC News, April 29, 2015, http://abcnews.go.com/Primetime/ story?id=132376&page=1.

11. "Sexual Health of Adolescents and Young Adults in the United States," The Henry J. Kaiser Foundation, August 20, 2014, http://kff.org/womens-health-policy/fact-sheet/sexual-health-of-adolescents-and-young-adults-in-the-united-states/.

12. Ibid.

13. "DrugFacts: High School and Youth Trends," National Institute on Drug Abuse, December 2014, https://www.drugabuse.gov/publications/drugfacts/ high-school-youth-trends.

14. Pekrun, R., Goetz, T., Daniels, L., Stupnisky, R., & Perry, R. "Boredom in Achievement Settings: Exploring Control-Value Antecedents and Performance Outcomes of a Neglected Emotion," *Journal of Educational Psychology*, 102(3), 531-549.

15. Ibid.

16. "The Test Chinese Schools Still Fail," *The Wall Street Journal*, December 8, 2010, http://www.wsj.com/ articles/SB100014240527487037667045760086924 93038646.

"Just as eating contrary to the inclination is injurious to the health, study without desire spoils the memory, and it retains nothing that it takes in."[1]

—LEONARDO DA VINCI

THREE

―⊶⊷―

LET'S TALK SOLUTIONS

H L. Mencken, a critic of the modern education system, argued that the ultimate goal of that system is to standardize the citizenry in order to suppress originality and eliminate dissent.[2] This is clearly a problem. Mencken also bitingly observed that, "There is always an easy solution to every human problem—neat, plausible, and wrong."[3] Can the worrisome issues identified in the first chapter be corrected, or are we resigned to a fate of failed attempts?

As this chapter will explain, each of the previously listed problems has a corresponding counterpart that parents can strive toward in order to provide a more meaningful and successful education for children. Mencken is perhaps right to note that *easy* proposals are often wrong, and (fair warning!) the ideas we'll consider in this chapter aren't easy. They require a significant investment of time and energy, both physical and mental, on the part of parents. What's important is that they are achievable and extremely beneficial for children. They are what education actually is once you remove all of the institutional, procedural, and logistical complications that reformers have introduced, and parents have accepted for too long.

INQUIRY, NOT INFORMATION

Children should be taught *how* to think, not *what* to think. And while professional educators would likely agree with this statement in principle, they find themselves working in a system that does not facilitate this basic tenet of teaching. In chapter one, we reviewed some of the problems involved in a schooling structure that emphasizes and rewards the learning and regurgitation of information. This test-centric method applauds children who arrive at a destination without ensuring that they will be able to find their own way there in the future.

The obvious solution to this problem is to equip our children with the ability to think critically—an important goal we established in the previous chapter. You may find yourself nodding your head in agreement but feeling confused as to how to actually pursue this goal. Fundamentally, it's a matter of inquiry over information—valuing the process of discovery as much, or more, than the result.

Put simply, we need to focus less on cramming a child's mind full of facts and figures, and more on how to ask questions that lead them to the truth. The right kind of question will do more to inspire your child and spark a serious study of a given subject than any number of fact sheets and documentaries. Reviewing information is primarily a passive activity; answering questions makes the child an active participant in the learning process. So what kinds of questions should we be asking?

Factual questions. Seeking knowledge often requires a preliminary review of the basic facts. Asking *who, what, when,* and *where* yields essential information that can lead to further understanding. What planets are in our solar system? Who was responsible for securing the independence of Scotland? When did the Boston Tea Party take place? Where is a person most likely to be able to see the Aurora Borealis? Each of these essential tidbits of data can then lead to a deeper inquiry.

Interpretive questions. Asking *why* and *how* requires a higher order of thinking—reflection and analysis that form the basis of critical thought. These questions can build on top of factual questions. Why do planets orbit around the sun? How was the independence of Scotland achieved? Why did so many people participate in the pre-Revolution protests in Boston? How does the Aurora Borealis work, and why are there different colors? These types of questions lead to contemplation, often revealing how little we know. Pondering interpretive questions can lead to genuine curiosity, which in turn motivates self-guided study.

Your child is more likely to develop a habit of critical thinking by asking them questions that are specifically designed to accomplish a few basic objectives, each of which encourages the learner to more deeply understand the answer being sought.

Compare and contrast. Something can often be understood best by pointing out its similarities and differences with things your child already understands. Why is gravity on the moon different than on Earth? Why hasn't there been another rebellion in America like there was in the 18th century against the British Empire? Why do the Romance languages have so many similar words? Asking questions designed to compare and contrast two things requires your child to seek an understanding of the characteristics of each thing. This increases observation and discernment.

Focus attention. Passively being taught information, such as listening to a presentation in a classroom, increases the likelihood that your child will become disengaged or distracted. Think of a daydreaming student who is suddenly asked a direct question by the teacher. That question immediately captures the student's attention and they find themselves required to respond (even if the answer is "I don't know"). Probing questions asked directly to your child will ensure that they are focused on the material and can dedicate their mental energy to the topic at hand.

Clarify to understand. New concepts explained to a child are often introduced superficially or simply. Invite your child to gain a deeper understanding by asking questions designed to increase their familiarity with the issue. For example, if you're discussing arithmetic you can ask your child to explain why 5 x 5 = 25 rather than having him simply memorize it, or explain why zero divided by any number is still zero. Again, we focus more on the process and understanding rather than simply arriving at and remembering the correct answer.

Make the learner the teacher. The Roman philosopher Seneca once stated, "While we teach, we learn."[4] Anybody who has had to prepare lesson material for school, church, or the workplace knows that they need to invest significant time and energy in order to master the material. Invite children to put themselves in the position of teacher by coming up with *their own* questions that will guide their study, rather than the parent being the source of all questioning. Invite them to then teach the material to a sibling, friend, or even you to unlock what's called "the protégé effect,"[5] where children learn better and retain more information by teaching it to others.

Children need a reason to care about the information they're learning. Give them context and purpose for what's being discussed by using probing questions designed to encourage critical thinking and a deeper understanding of the subjects that interest them. A child's mind is more than a mere storage container. Put it to work by enabling them to become masters of their own learning.

EDUCATIONAL FREEDOM

When I woke up on the day I wrote this subsection of the book, I received a Facebook notification from a group of fellow parents, most of whom (but not all) homeschool their children. The person posting, Rachel (I've changed her name to maintain privacy), published a raw, emotional plea for help from other parents. She described feeling overwhelmed, stressed out, unhappy, and had convinced herself that she was a failure. "Do I change curriculum?" she asked. "Be more organized? Be less structured?"

Rachel is certainly not the only parent to feel burned out and defeated from weeks, months, or years of conflict with a child. Forcing a son or daughter to do homework or complete a lesson or read a book when they don't want to establishes an environment of animosity and resentment—hardly a frame of mind that's conducive to curiosity and inquiry. There are inherent and pervasive problems in any education methodology that requires children to be subject to rigid structure and mandated curriculum.

The obvious solution to this is educational freedom—the elimination, or at least the reduction, of the structure that confines and constricts children. And, as it turns out, that was the recommendation of many of the fellow moms commenting in reply to Rachel's heartfelt plea. Here is a small (and lightly edited) sampling of responses she received:

- "I think if it is too structured and your children are forced to do work that may not be necessary, or could be taught a different way, that might be the source of conflict. I know it is with us."

- "I'm so sorry, I know that feeling too. But it only comes when I try to force my children to do something that they aren't ready for. Your kids are young. Play, explore, have fun with them! Teach them things you are learning during mealtimes and on walks in nature. Pray for teaching moments and be sneaky about it. Just play with them for a little while, you'll be amazed at how much better it feels."

- "I have had to adapt how we structure our day differently to accommodate the nature of my kids, and their relative ages. When we did too much structured time in our day, everyone—including me—was burned out. One thing that really has helped us was simplifying the school work."

• "Don't give up. One step at a time. Don't try too hard to stick to a schedule."

• "One thing that has helped me is taking time to decide what I want for my children. What do you want your children to know and who do you want them to be? Do you want them to love reading or do you just want them to read? Do you want them to love science or should they have facts crammed into their minds? We often try to recreate school at home without realizing we are recreating what we don't want for our children."

Every child is unique. This is something that any parent of two or more children understands, and something that is obvious when we look at society as a whole. Children have diverse interests and abilities, so why in the world would we expect them to learn the same information in the same way? Imagine how silly it would be to propose that all adults should read the same books or work in the same career. We wouldn't want to take the family to the beach if we had to do the same activities as every other family, and in the same location. We would avoid any restaurant that offered the same meal to every customer. Can't we give children the same space to be unique that we expect to be given as adults?

The main obstacle to allowing children to pursue their own educational interests is that for many it necessarily means that government and private schools are eliminated as options, unless they can facilitate complete customization of the child's curriculum. (As we'll see in the next chapter, that's not entirely out of the question.) In the United States, government mandates regarding education standards and testing leave parents who wish for their children to engage in passion-driven education little option other than to withdraw from these institutions and commit to homeschooling. Admittedly, not every family can accommodate having one parent remain at home with the children (especially in the case of single parents), and not every state allows homeschooled children to be educated without required curricula and tests. But even in these situations, parents can make a concerted effort to use a child's free time, outside of existing educational requirements, to inspire them and allow them to learn about the things that interest them.

An example of one teacher who managed to implement education freedom in his public school classroom to great success is Sergio Juárez Correa, a teacher at the José Urbina López Primary School in Matamoros, Mexico, a dangerous and impoverished town near the U.S. border. His elementary school class had unreliable electricity, few resources, spotty Internet access, and sometimes not enough to eat. "But you do have one thing that makes you the equal of any kid in the world," he told his students. "Potential."[6] Having recently become convinced that his previous top-down teaching style was not yielding any success, Correa decided to switch things up. "From now on, we're going to use that potential to make you the best students in the world." He looked around the room and revolutionized the lives of those students by asking a single, simple question:

"What do you want to learn?"

The results were astounding. During the previous year, 45% of the students failed the math portion of their annual assessment, and 31% failed Spanish. Now, only 7% failed math and 3.5% failed Spanish. Whereas no student had received an "Excellent" score in the past, 63% now achieved that classification in math. When the school's assistant principal reviewed the scores, he was surprised and impressed:

> The language scores were very high. Even the lowest was well above the national average. Then he noticed the math scores. The top score in [Correa's] class was 921. [The assistant principal] looked over at the top score in the state: It was 921. When he saw the next box over, the hairs on his arms stood up. The top score in the entire country was also 921.[7]

That top score in the entire country belonged to Paloma Bueno, a shy 12-year-old girl in Correa's class.

When he realized that Paloma was clearly gifted in math, Correa wanted to know why she hadn't expressed much interest in it previously. Her reply? "Because no one made it this interesting." She wasn't the only one: the student-led method of learning that Correa employed in his classroom put ten other students right behind Paloma in math, each falling within the 99.99th percentile. He had provided his students the freedom to learn what they wanted in the way they wanted, and the results were profound.

It would be difficult to replicate Correa's process and achieve the same results in the United States. Teachers are bound by rigid guidelines and find themselves teaching the content for which students will be tested, rather than what they desire to learn. Enabling students to learn about their passions can certainly be done in a group setting, and even in schools, but it is much more likely to occur in the home where children are shielded from the controlling oversight of classrooms and an overwhelming obsession with standardized testing.

Children need the ability to explore the world around them in ways that satisfy their curiosity and help them make sense of their world. The freedom to have a say in what they learn, and when and how it's studied, is an empowering gift that will increase a child's sense of independence and excitement in their educational efforts. Coercing our children to study an off-the-shelf, one-size-fits-all curriculum, during arbitrary times of the day and with mandated assignments, does not provide them the tools and time necessary to learn the things that interest them in the way that suits them best.

INDIVIDUALIZATION

Factory processes and the manufacturing model of the modern education system have industrialized a process that, ideally, should be customized to the individual child. Each person's uniqueness means that they will be interested and proficient in different subjects, yet millions upon millions of children are placed on the same conveyor belt that washes away their individuality in favor of conformity and a homogenous, predictable output.

The obvious solution to this problem is to remove your child from the conveyor belt and avoid any industrialized, one-size-fits-all systems or standards that fail to respect and accommodate your child's uniqueness.

I firmly believe that my children have a purpose in life—a path that God knows and has prepared for them. I have no clue what that is, and they don't yet know either. But if anybody will figure it out, it's them, possibly with insight from me and my wife as their parents. It definitely won't be a textbook manufacturer who has had its content dictated to them by government curriculum committees. I don't want to imprint some arbitrary societal standard onto my children. I don't want them to become a miniature version of their parents, learning and doing what we know and do. Their path may be completely different. To find that path, they'll need the freedom to wander and experiment and explore the things that interest them in the moment their attention is hooked. Confining children to a classroom and bombarding them with assignments renders that ideal extremely difficult, if not impossible.

Good parents already understand this. We identify what our children's abilities are, and then encourage them to expand them or acquire new ones. We pay attention to our children's interests and enable them to pursue their curiosities. We know where they are, and help them take one small step further, over and over again. Unfortunately, some parents still subject their children to lesson plans or assignments against their will, imposing an authoritarian requirement on the student. Sometimes this is out of a conscious necessity—in the case of parents who want an individual approach for their children but cannot provide it, given their family's circumstances—but too often it is a decision borne of ignorance or wanting their children to "fit in" and attend school like everybody else.

This is part of a larger issue—that of individualism versus collectivism. Under an individualist method of organizing society, each person is independent and free to pursue their own interests and desires. They have unalienable rights that are respected and protected. They control their own destiny and need only ensure that as they embark in their "pursuit of happiness" they do not harm another person or violate their rights in the process. Collectivism, on the other hand, places the supposed interests of society before those of the individual; what matters is the whole, and not necessarily any individual part. A select few are placed in charge of determining how to organize the affairs of the many in an attempt to realize the greater good.

As it pertains to children, the collectivist mindset can be found in industrialized education systems that encourage commonality and require standardized learning. All must learn the same things and be given the same opportunities. The very name of the "Common Core" standards clearly reflects its support for collectivism. Government departments of education, school boards, curriculum committees—these and other centralized institutions of power and influence give a platform for central planners to create systems and processes that they can impose on the masses. Rightly did George Orwell note that collectivism "gives to a tyrannical minority such powers as the Spanish Inquisitors never dreamt of"[8]—in this case, the power to shape the opinions and beliefs of the rising generation. Parents are considered to be mere procreators and breadwinners; others know what is best for a child's future, and therefore what they need to learn.

The individualist mindset, however, sets aside these systems to focus specifically on your unique child. Parents are considered the resident experts for their children; no elected official, bureaucrat, or financially incentivized curriculum salesman knows better than you. The needs and interests of your child are paramount, and all educational efforts should be catered to and customized for him or her. We can certainly use books, worksheets, lesson plans, and other prepared materials as a support should our child show interest, but we make sure that the curriculum conforms to the child's interests, rather than coercing the child to conform to the curriculum.

Practically speaking, what individualized education entails is creating a plan based around the current abilities and interests of your child. If your child is struggling to understand division or photosynthesis or the fall of the Roman Empire, then slow down, take it easy, and perhaps approach it from a different angle. There should be no artificial timelines or expectations. And if your child is mastering a subject more easily, then push harder, go deeper, and let him or her plow through the material at whatever speed is most comfortable.

This child-specific plan isn't just about the speed with which material is learned. An individualized plan also means that some subjects won't be studied in any significant way. The simple truth that most parents don't want to embrace is that not every child has to learn long division, the anatomical names of key body parts, or the names of each state capital. Not every child needs to comprehend the same information at the same age. It could very well be that your child is completely disinterested in, say, geometry—and that's fine. Industrialized education aims to ensure a homogenous result requiring every child to learn a variety of subjects, most of which they'll quickly forget and never use later in their lives. If we're focusing on our child's interests and needs, we should be careful to avoid this collectivist approach.

Children need the opportunity to learn what interests them in the way that best suits them. They need parents and trusted teachers and mentors to guide them and provide access to resources and educational materials that satisfy their curiosity and match their interests. Let's respect their individuality by providing them a customized education experience that helps them find and follow their unique path in life.

THE FARMING MODEL

Deference to authority permeates our society—elected officials, doctors, police officers, religious leaders, and teachers often can control the behavior and thoughts of others by virtue of their position. Individuals outsource their thinking to others, content to go along with their decisions—after all, officials and leaders wouldn't hold those positions if they didn't know best. This authoritarianism is clearly visible in the modern education system, where rather than being built upon a foundation of critical thinkers and facilitating inquiry and customization of curriculum, the system is suspended from its apex—government bureaucracies and curriculum committees produce required material that is then pushed down onto everyone below.

The obvious solution to this problem is to provide our children an education experience that is individual to their needs and driven largely by them—a bottom-up, natural system in which they are at the helm. More importantly, we as parents need to create and maintain an environment in which our children have the greatest opportunity to thrive. This vision was articulated in an excellent TED talk by Sir Ken Robinson, a popular public speaker and education advisor:

> We have to go from what is essentially an industrial model of education, a manufacturing model, which is based on linearity and conformity and batching people. We have to move to a model that is based more on principles of agriculture. We have to recognize that human flourishing is not a mechanical process—it's an organic process. And you cannot predict the outcome of human development. All you can do, like a farmer, is create the conditions under which they will begin to flourish.[9]

Chapter one established that schools are factories, unable and unwilling to adapt to and serve the interests of your children. If the solution to those problems means having to homeschool, then what can caring parents do to "create the conditions under which [their children] will begin to flourish"? How can your children thrive if removed from the institutions that were theoretically created to support them? In addition to the other solutions mentioned in this chapter, there are a few additional steps a parent can take—actions based on the principles of agriculture:

Put your child in the driver's seat. As Correa did for his impoverished classroom of students in Mexico, simply ask your child what he or she would like to learn. Allowing a person to control their own destiny—even a young child—affirms their individuality, respects their interests, and encourages them to think more clearly about their short- and long-term future. Recognize that just as a plant has DNA designed to control its development, your child has a future that will reveal itself as the right circumstances are provided.

Provide your child with resources. If your son wants to learn about giraffes, then go to the zoo and ask to speak with one of the workers who cares for that animal to allow your son to get his questions answered. If your daughter likes astronomy, buy a telescope, visit a museum, or rent a related documentary. This positions parents not as the sources of information, but as facilitators—adults with access to people, products, and services that can satisfy the child's curiosity and enable them to learn more about what interests them. Farmers fret more over the resources available to their plants than they do the plants themselves, because they know that if a plant is provided with proper nutrients, sun, and water, it will largely take care of the rest. Our focus, as parents, should be on making sure that our child has what he or she needs and desires to pursue his or her educational interests.

Don't do it alone. The single most common feeling among parents who homeschool is burnout—a mixed sensation of stress, despair, and inadequacy. It makes no sense to educate your child in isolation! Join a commonwealth or co-op with other families in your situation. If there are none in your area, start your own or associate with like-minded families online to share ideas and receive support. This network will help both parent and child through increased exposure to others who are more experienced and who can help with specific challenges. Farmers often share tips and equipment with one another, and often exchange labor during different harvest seasons. Even though it's your child, you're not in this alone—reach out for help and develop a support network.

Get out of the way. As a parent facilitator, your job is not to have all the answers to your child's questions. Chances are, they will develop an interest in a subject in which you have little to no expertise. For that reason, it's important to identify and network with adult mentors who can help your child. If your daughter is interested in learning a programming language, find a neighbor, family member, or friend who works in that field and can take her under their wing. If your son likes airplanes, find a pilot who can answer his aviation questions and expose him to others in that industry. Sometimes the mentor might be found on a pre-recorded lecture series or through a self-taught online course. For older children, mentors are an extremely influential resource that will accelerate your child's education and professional development. Just as farmers often rely on the knowledge of others who are more experienced in pesticide use, grafting, or crop rotation, parents should seek support from experts and experienced individuals in the subjects that interest their child.

Children need a holistic process that focuses on the circumstances surrounding their customized education. Once provided, parents will have the benefit of watching them naturally flourish, just as a farmer watches in awe and wonder at a plant growing and thriving once it is given access to basic resources. This attention to detail will take effort on your part. As Robinson noted,

"Human resources are like natural resources; they're often buried deep. You have to go looking for them. They're not just lying around on the surface. You have to create the circumstances where they show themselves."[10] But if you've ever had a garden or orchard, you know the satisfying feeling of watching nature take its course, and later being able to harvest the delicious results. Let's give our children the information, tools, and environment they need to naturally thrive.

AGE MIXING

Contrary to natural family dynamics and the socio-behavioral history of every culture on the planet, the modern education system compels children to interact with and learn alongside others of their same age. These arbitrary and forced relationships minimize diversity, increase competitiveness, and remove opportunities for children with different levels of knowledge, ability, and maturity to positively influence and support your child.

The obvious solution to this problem is to steer clear of educational institutions that rely on age segregation as a method of organizing children into groups or classes. As a part of their educational experience, your child should not be denied the opportunity to reap the benefits of age mixing, which are many. Peter Gray, a psychologist and education researcher who has written extensively on how age mixing benefits a child's development, offers six examples of these benefits—three for younger children and three for older children.[11] They are as follows:

Age mixing allows younger children to play within their zones of proximal development. This term, coined in the 1930s by Russian psychologist Lev Vygostsky, refers to the type of activities that a young child cannot do alone or with others at their level, but can do when being helped by older children or adults who are competent in that activity. Exposure to older children allows a young child to participate in, learn about, and benefit from more advanced activities just outside their comfort zone. To demonstrate this, Gray documented age-mixed recreation among children aged four to ten, identifying many instances in which young children were introduced to numerical concepts beyond their ability to understand. Gray writes:

> In one example, an older child explained how to give exactly seven drops of medicine—no more and no less—to a sick doll. In another, during a game of store, an older child explained to a younger one how much it costs to purchase two items in the case where one costs ten dollars and the other five dollars and how much change to give for a twenty-dollar bill. Such concepts appear far more meaningful to children in their own, self-directed pretend play than in the more abstract and less voluntary setting of typical classroom instruction.[12]

Age mixing provides the younger children with models to emulate. Just as I learned to write well by imitating experienced and successful authors, children often learn through observation and emulation. The authors of *The Anthropology of Learning in Childhood* contend at the outset of their book that "[t]he single most important form of learning is observation."[13] Gray notes that traditional societies feature very little explicit teaching; children practice new skills by observation and practicing with others who are more advanced than they are. He continues:

> Children learn about their world through exploration, and they consolidate that information—both verbally and in motor patterns—in their play. The biggest part of exploration for children is observing other human beings, especially those who are older, more skilled, and more knowledgeable. Such observations include hearing as well as watching. Children attend to the conversations and actions of older children and adults, and they incorporate what they see and hear into their own play.[14]

Age mixing provides younger children with additional sources of care and emotional support. Parents of teenagers often recognize that positive relationships their children develop with other adults can be helpful emotionally and developmentally. Non-familial mentors provide teenagers with a "sounding board" and support system outside of the parent-child relationship who can validate or supplement what is taught and experienced in the home. This same idea extends to younger children, who can benefit from having older non-sibling children help and encourage them. There have been few studies conducted to analyze this aspect of non-sibling peer support, but Gray explains what one of them found after analyzing mixed-age tutoring in a school setting, where eighth graders taught first graders three times a week for twenty minutes at a time:

> The researchers observed that at first the tutors spent most of their tutoring time trying to keep their tutees on task but that, by the end of the first month, the relationships became more playful and affectionate. The first graders began sitting on their tutors' laps, and there was a marked increase in such signs of affection as handholding... head-patting, and good-natured banter. According to the researchers, the relationships that best satisfied the affective needs and desires of the first graders were also the most successful in meeting the cognitive goals of the tutoring program.[15]

Age mixing allows older children to develop their capacities to nurture and lead. Many children—especially those with older siblings—quickly grow tired of their role as the inexperienced or immature member of the family. Exposure to younger children, especially in an educational setting, offers them an opportunity to be the mature one in a relationship and develop leadership and nurturing qualities. Especially when they have their own positive role models, they can incorporate and emulate what they have learned from being the recipient of someone else's guidance. Gray explains the research on this topic:

> Cross-age tutoring studies in Western schools commonly reveal increases in measures of responsibility, empathy, and altruism in the tutors. Researchers have also found, not surprisingly, that children exert much more leadership when they collaborate with younger children in joint tasks than when they collaborate with age-mates.[16]

Age mixing allows older children to expand their understanding through teaching. As established earlier, those who are asked to teach a concept are more likely to seek greater understanding of it. If confined with others of their same age, a child's tutoring opportunities are reduced only to those who are struggling with the concept—but who may resist being tutored by a peer for fear of being perceived as unintelligent. Younger children naturally are "behind" an older child in age and development, so older children are more easily able to teach them. This experience forces the older child to understand a concept well enough to articulate it to the younger child, as Gray explains:

> When older children explain concepts to younger ones in age-mixed play, they must turn their previously implicit, unstated knowledge into words

that younger children can understand. For example, the eight-year-old explaining to the two-year-old the steps in bathing a baby, in their combined doll play, may have been putting those steps into words, and thinking about them verbally for the first time. Likewise, children helping others learn to read or to use numbers in the context of play are, most likely, making certain phonetic or numeric concepts clearer to themselves as they explain them and answer the questions of younger children.[17]

Age mixing fosters creativity in older children. Just as tutoring opportunities decrease in same-age situations, competitiveness increases. By equalizing age, children want to outshine their peers by way of personality, knowledge, or skill. By mixing ages, this instinct is minimized and opportunities for complementary participation increase, and children with differing abilities, talents, or ideas can work together, rather than against one another. Gray writes:

> When children all nearly of the same age play a game, competitiveness can interfere with playfulness. This is especially true in our modern, Western culture, which puts so much emphasis on winning and on all sorts of comparisons aimed at determining who is better. In contrast, when children of widely different ages play a game together, the focus shifts from winning to having fun. There is no pride to be gained by the older, larger, more-skilled child in beating the much younger one, and the younger one has no

expectation of beating the older one. So, they play
the game more joyfully, in a more relaxed manner,
modifying the rules to make the game both fun and
challenging, but not overwhelming, for all.[18]

Children need exposure to, and support from, a
wide range of peers whose perspective, background,
and knowledge can aid them along their own path. John
Taylor Gatto writes that the modern education system
"effectively cuts you off from the immense diversity of
life and the synergy of variety; indeed it cuts you off from
your own past and future, scaling you to a continuous
present..."[19] Let's provide our children with the benefits
of "the immense diversity of life" by ensuring that their
educational experience does not reduce their ability to
interact with and learn from children of other ages.

ENDNOTES

1. Leonardo da Vinci, *Leonardo's Notebooks: Writing and Art of the Great Master* (New York: Black Dog & Leventhal Publishers, Inc., 2005), 392.

2. H.L. Mencken, "The Little Red Schoolhouse," *The American Mercury*, vol. 1, (New York: Alfred Knoff, 1924) 504.

3. H.L. Mencken, *A Mencken Chrestomathy* (New York: Vintage Books, 1982), 443.

4. Roger L'Estrange, ed., *Seneca's Morals* (London: W. Bowyer, 17p2), 225.

5. "Teachable Agents and the Protégé Effect: Increasing the Effort Towards Learning," *Journal of Science Education and Technology*, vol. 18, issue 4 , 334-352.

6. "A Radical Way of Unleashing a Generation of Geniuses," *Wired*, October 15, 2013, http://www.wired.com/2013/10/free-thinkers/.

7. Ibid.

8. Sonia Orwell, ed., *George Orwell: As I Please, 1943-1946* (Boston: Nonpareil Books, 2000), 118.

9. "Bring on the learning revolution!," TED, February 2010, https://www.ted.com/talks/sir_ken_robinson_bring_on_the_revolution/.

10. Ibid.
11. Peter Gray, "The Special Value of Children's Age-Mixed Play," *American Journal of Play*, vol. 3, no. 4. (2011), 500-522.
12. Ibid.
13. David F. Lancy, John Bock, and Suzanne Gaskins, "Putting Learning into Context," in *The Anthropology of Learning in Childhood* (2010), 5.
14. Peter Gray, "The Special Value of Children's Age-Mixed Play."
15. Ibid.
16. Ibid.
17. Ibid.
18. Ibid.
19. John Taylor Gatto, "Why Schools Don't Educate," The Natural Child Project, http://www.naturalchild.org/guest/john_gatto.html.

"A general state education is a mere contrivance for molding people to be exactly like one another. Since the mold in which it casts them is that which pleases the predominant power in the government—whether this be a monarch, a priesthood, an aristocracy, or the majority of the existing generation—in proportion as it is efficient and successful, it establishes a despotism over the mind, leading by natural tendency to one over the body. An education established and controlled by the state should only exist, if it exists at all, as one among many competing experiments, carried on for the purpose of example and stimulus to keep the others up to a certain standard of excellence."[1]

—JOHN STUART MILL

FOUR

❦

A DIFFERENT WAY

In the film *Dead Poets Society*, the inspiring teacher, John Keating, tells his students that they "must constantly look at things in a different way." He continues:

> Just when you think you know something, you have to look at it in another way. Even though it may seem silly or wrong, you must try! Dare to strike out and find new ground.[2]

Keating's encouragement to gain a different perspective was the key influence behind Apple's highly successful advertising campaign in 1997. Steve Jobs, the company's legendary founder, had been pushed out of the company over a decade earlier. Since his departure, Apple had floundered, sales had lagged, and the media had lost interest. Executives had dumped more than half a billion dollars into a failed attempt to create the Newton, a personal digital assistant, and had bled the company of hundreds of millions of dollars in unsuccessful marketing in an attempt to revitalize the company's image.

Jobs returned to Apple and gained control, immediately embarking on a mission to change public perception of his company. The marketing campaign Jobs launched was reflective of his vision and goal—the very reason why he founded Apple in the first place. The flagship commercial for the campaign featured images of a variety of iconic figures as Richard Dreyfuss read these words:

Here's to the crazy ones.

The misfits. The rebels. The troublemakers. The round pegs in the square holes.

The ones who see things differently.

They're not fond of rules. And they have no respect for the status quo.

You can quote them, disagree with them, glorify or vilify them. About the only thing you can't do is ignore them.

Because they change things. They push the human race forward.

And while some see them as the crazy ones, we see genius.

Because the people who are crazy enough to think they can change the world, are the ones who do.

Apple's campaign captured the public's imagination and tapped into our collective desire to be inspired. The company revitalized its image and reinvigorated its employees whose innovative products soon thereafter birthed a generation of creative rebels and pioneers of entirely new industries that have revolutionized the world. Apple's campaign, harkening back to *Dead Poets Society*, was titled, "Think Different."

It is time for parents to "think different."

Most don't. It's extremely common to accept the status quo and do what nearly everybody else is doing. But now, you likely understand that the status quo is unacceptable and that children are not meant for a conveyor belt. Keating told his students, "Despite what anyone might tell you, words and ideas can change the world." He's right. And as it pertains to education—to your child's development and future—the transformational idea is freedom. It's an idea that has toppled authoritarian governments, unleashed innovative products and services to improve our quality of life, and motivated millions of people throughout world history—and it can and will motivate your child. Freedom is the basis for what you'll read about in the remainder of this book.

Having outlined the problems and proposed some solutions, I imagine you probably have several questions: How can I take these ideas and implement them in our family? Do I have to homeschool my child? Can

I really trust my son or daughter to direct their own education? What would any of this look like on a day-to-day basis? Will my child be prepared adequately for adulthood?

What most parents crave as they abandon the modern education system is an outline they can follow—it's why so many families cling to curricula where the thinking, prioritization, and process are pre-packaged and spoon-fed to the student. This chapter will introduce several alternative, non-curricular education methods—ways to "think different" about your approach. Yet they are each a variation on a theme—different implementations of the fundamental principle of basing education on a child's interests.

MINIMALLY INVASIVE EDUCATION

The success of Sergio Correa's students as described in the previous chapter was not the result of mere happenstance. During his five years as a teacher, Correa had been following the mandated curriculum to the letter, bored out of his mind and believing it was a waste of both his and the students' time. He decided that things needed to change.

When Correa flipped education on its head and offered to let his class take the lead, he was incorporating a fascinating idea he had encountered that had been developed by Sugata Mitra, a professor of educational technology in the United Kingdom. Mitra's educational campaign began in 1999, when he was a scientist working at a software development company in New Delhi. The company's building bordered a slum. Acting on a whim, he set up a computer in a hole in the wall facing the slum, curious to see how the impoverished children nearby would react. No instructor, no lesson manual, no notes—just a computer. To his astonishment, and with no prior experience, the children were able to teach themselves how to use it.

This "hole in the wall" experiment, as it's come to be known, was soon replicated in other villages throughout India. Over 300 "learning stations" have been used by hundreds of thousands of children; the initial experiment's results have been repeatedly reproduced. But the experiments aren't just limited to computer literacy; Mitra's efforts grew more ambitious over time.

In 2010, Mitra set up a computer in a tiny village in southern India, loading it with information on molecular biology. He encouraged a small group of pre-teens to explore the computer and suggested they might find the computer and its contents interesting. Then, he left— offering no advice, input, or orientation that would benefit the children. The results were remarkable:

> Over the next 75 days, the children worked out how to use the computer and began to learn. When

Mitra returned, he administered a written test on molecular biology. The kids answered about one in four questions correctly. After another 75 days, with the encouragement of a friendly local, they were getting every other question right.[3]

"If you put a computer in front of children and remove all other adult restrictions, they will self-organize around it," Mitra says, "like bees around a flower."[4] It's an interesting phenomenon, given the level of ignorance these children begin with at the outset of the experiment. Mitra believes that a new education methodology is possible in the Information Age, due to the ease with which knowledge can be obtained by anybody with access to the Internet.

Correa's adoption of this child-centric method, answering curiosity and questions with the help of abundantly available information through an Internet-connected device, brought tremendous results. Building on the success of his experiments, Mitra is opening up schools "in the cloud," where students explore what interests them while in class by researching the answers online. They are guided by remotely located mentors who are available to the students through a video chat.

Known as "minimally invasive education," this self-directed learning process can be applied both in the home and in the classroom. All that is needed is access to resources through which the child can explore and learn, and a parent or mentor who can respond to questions or help the child overcome any insurmountable obstacles they encounter. "Working in small groups, children can competently search for answers to 'big questions', drawing rational, logical conclusions," explains Dr. Suneeta Kulkarni, research director for Mitra's School in the Cloud project. "This is far ahead of what is expected of them in their school curriculum and a kind of learning activated by questions, not answers."[5]

UNSCHOOLING

While Sugata Mitra's experiments brought important attention to the legitimacy of self-directed learning, they were predated by a group of radicals during the hippie era. Sudbury Valley School, founded in Massachusetts in 1968, created an institutionalized environment "founded upon the principle that learning is best fostered by self-motivation, self-regulation, and self-criticism..."[6] The school implements what Mitra calls minimally invasive education, or what is now popularly referred to as "unschooling."

Sudbury Valley School enrolls up to 200 students, with children spanning the ages between four and 18. A few adults are employed to maintain the school and respond to questions asked by the students, but they remain on staff at the discretion of the students themselves who, no matter their age, each have a single vote in a democratic governance model. There are no administered tests, no attendance requirements, and no grades. There are a wide range of supplies and resources in the school, but their use is optional. Children wander and act freely on the ten acres of property. They play, read, talk, socialize—they do whatever interests them. And the adults wait in the wings for children to demonstrate interest and ask for help. Their credo, according to Daniel Greenberg, one of the school's founders, is "Wait for the student to take the first step."[7]

This amount of freedom terrifies many parents. How do you know your child is learning without measuring improvement through tests? What happens if they play video games all day long, or spend the day fishing in the nearby lake? "This is the leap of faith, the swan dive off the mountain into thin air," says Heather Haskins, a parent with two young children attending Tallgrass Sudbury—one of over 60 schools modeled after the original.[8]

But that's not quite true. Studies of Sudbury graduates indicate that children who direct their own education under this model confirm a high range of personal satisfaction along with placement in a wide range of careers—engineers, small business owners, doctors, and everything in between. Graduates desiring to enter college had no problem doing so, and the choices of

Sudbury graduates in both career and college reflected similar results seen among public high school graduates.[9] In regard to the final question in one survey he conducted, psychologist Peter Gray notes, "None of the graduates said that their life would be better if they had attended a traditional school rather than Sudbury Valley."[10] That's an approval rating you would never find in public school.

Greenberg has written extensively about the philosophy behind this unique approach, what it's actually like for the participating children, and what the results are. In describing why he and the school's other founders modeled it the way they did, he offers the following:

> We felt that the only learning that ever counts in life happens when the learners have thrown themselves into a subject on their own, without coaxing, or bribing, or pressure....

> We knew that people would make mistakes this way—but they would know that the mistakes they made are their own, and so they would be likelier to learn from them.[11]

Age mixing is the so-called "secret weapon"[12] of Sudbury; in one study, over half of the interactions were among children whose ages differed by more than two years, and in a quarter of them, there was an age difference of over four years.[13] Greenberg explains the effect of age mixing at his school:

The principle is always the same: if anyone wants to do something, they do it. Interest is what counts. If the activity is on an advanced level, skill counts. A lot of little kids are much more skillful than older ones at a lot of things.

When the skills and rate of learning aren't all on the same level, that's when the fun begins. The kids help each other. They have to, otherwise the group as a whole will fall behind. They want to, because they are not competing for grades or gold stars. They like to, because it's terribly satisfying to help someone else and succeed at it.[14]

These schools tend to cost around $8,000-10,000 per year for a child to attend, but the basic concept of allowing children the freedom to pursue their interests at their own pace can be implemented in the home. The very name itself, unschooling, suggests that it is better defined by what it isn't, rather than explaining what it is. Schools (including the in-the-home variety) have classes or curricula with differentiated subjects; unschooling doesn't. Schools have goals set by the teacher; unschooling doesn't. Schools have specific learning materials provided; unschooling doesn't. Schooling is structured; unschooling isn't.

Put simply, unschooling involves providing an opportunity for a child to explore his or her interests. It's also important that there be consequences; for example, if your son decides to play video games all week, the inevitable feeling of lethargy may provide a good teaching opportunity to suggest alternative uses of his time the following week. Life itself is a learning environment in unschooling; your role is not that of teacher but of facilitator, providing your children, as much as possible, with the resources necessary to answer the questions they come up with. Unschooling is not unparenting; children should still be encouraged and exposed to positive and interesting information and ideas. However, if the child shows no interest, the unschooling parent backs off and waits, potentially taking a new approach in the future to encourage interest in the subject.

Educational resources for unschoolers can include the very curricula or textbooks you might think should be totally abandoned. John Holt, a prolific educator popular within the unschooling movement, explains:

> Unschooling, for lack of a better term (until people start to accept living as part and parcel of learning), is the natural way to learn. However, this does not mean unschoolers do not take traditional classes or use curricular materials when the student, or parents and children together, decide that this is how they want to do it. Learning to read or do quadratic equations are not "natural" processes, but unschoolers nonetheless learn them when it makes sense to them to do so, not because they have reached a certain age or are compelled to do so by arbitrary authority. Therefore it isn't unusual to find unschoolers

who are barely eight-years-old studying astronomy
or who are ten-years-old and just learning to read.

Just as legitimate governments operate with the consent of the governed, unschooling affirms that legitimate educational systems require the interest of the student. Once your child is interested in a subject, you don't need to force anything. It's more likely that you'll be brainstorming ways to get him or her to spend less time so focused on that subject.

While traditional homeschooling is stressful for parents who presume they must be universal subject matter experts for their children, unschooling is a relaxing and natural approach—one that allows parents to be themselves, and co-learners with their curious children. As Greenberg said of Sudbury, "The recipe is simple: one part freedom, one part dignity, one part responsibility, one part support, mix together and let sit until ready. Any chef can copy it with the same success."[15]

A THOMAS JEFFERSON EDUCATION

Thomas Paine's *Common Sense* took colonial America by storm, selling over 120,000 copies in its first three months of publication. While that number seems high on its own, it would be the equivalent of selling around 15 million copies in the United States of America based on the current population. After its first year, nearly 500,000 copies were sold—enough for around 20% of the entire population to own a copy. That's the equivalent of 60 million copies in today's numbers—and after only one year. For some perspective, the book that reached 60 million in sales the fastest in modern times was *The Da Vinci Code*, but it took eight years for it to reach that milestone.

What's more interesting is the prose contained in *Common Sense*—it's more complex English than what school children (and adults) are used to today. Consider this paragraph from the book's introduction:

> As a long and violent abuse of power is generally the means of calling the right of it in question (and in matters too which might never have been thought of, had not the sufferers been aggravated into the inquiry) and as the king of England hath undertaken in his *own right*, to support the parliament in what he calls *theirs*, and as the good people of this country are grievously oppressed by the combination, they have an undoubted privilege to inquire into the pretensions of both, and equally to reject the usurpations of either.[16]

That's some meaty material to chew on. The fact that such a complicated essay was still so popular suggests that people were not uneducated before the rise of the modern education system. But according to a survey by the National Assessment of Adult Literacy, only 13%

of adult Americans have achieved an adequate level of proficiency to comprehend *Common Sense*.[17]

Oliver DeMille, a bestselling author and educator, wanted to understand how the framers of the U.S. Constitution were educated. His studies focused on Thomas Jefferson—a brilliant man whose knowledge spanned many areas and several languages. Jefferson was a perpetual student, and under the tutelage of George Wythe—the first law professor in America— he burst onto the scene as one of the country's greatest leaders. DeMille's study has resulted in an education model he called, quite appropriately, "A Thomas Jefferson Education." In a book by the same name, he explains how this style of study relies heavily on mentors, both living and long since deceased:

> There are two types of great teachers which consistently motivate student-driven education: Mentors and Classics. Mentors meet face-to-face with the student, inspiring through the transfer of knowledge, the force of personality, and individual attention. Classics were created by other great teachers to be experienced in books, art, music and other media.[18]

Students following this model can customize their list of "classics"—works of literature, music, or art that are worth repeatedly reviewing because you learn something new, or gain more value, each time. DeMille's recommendations are broken into different developmental ages, or "phases," that are loosely assigned based on a child's intellectual and emotional readiness.

TJEd, as it's abbreviated, highlights "Seven Keys of Great Teaching": classics, not textbooks; mentors, not professors; inspire, not require; structure time, not content; quality, not conformity; simplicity, not complexity; and you, not them. This model bases a child's educational experience on the issues, ideas, and training necessary to become a future community leader, entrepreneur, or statesman—a person of worth who contributes to society.

In his later years, Thomas Jefferson wrote a letter to his son, expressing concern for his grandson's education. Jefferson offered his opinion that a structured curriculum that led to a degree would not be the best use of his grandson's time, and suggested instead that he should focus on a course of study that would be better suited for his individual interests. "This relinquishes the honorary distinction of a diploma, a good enough thing to excite the ambition of youth to study," Jefferson wrote, "but in modern estimation, no longer worth tacking, by its initials even, to one's name; and certainly not worth the sacrifice of a single useful science."[19] Jefferson's suggestion, put simply, was to focus on material that mattered—not that which led to arbitrary acronyms after one's name, or a piece of paper.

True leaders don't care about such trappings of academia anyway.

THE MONTESSORI METHOD

Maria Montessori, an Italian physician, found herself in a Roman asylum for the insane in 1897 seeking patients for treatment at her clinic. A caretaker approached her and related how disgusted she was to see the children grab crumbs off the floor after their meal. The complaint merely made Montessori curious, and she concluded that the children—who were kept in a bare, unfurnished environment—were desperate for stimuli to activate their senses. They were sensory deprived.

Dr. Montessori developed a side interest in pedagogy—the study of how best to teach. While her early research focused on the intellectually and developmentally disabled, she soon began applying her educational theories to "normal" children. Montessori concluded that, like those in the asylum, all children desire environmental interactivity—learning by manipulating things with their hands:

> The child cannot develop if he does not have objects around him permitting him to act. Until the present, it was believed that the most effective learning took place when knowledge was passed on directly to the child by his teachers. But it is really the environment that is the best teacher. The child needs objects to act; they are like nourishment for his spirit.[20]

Montessori opened a *Casa dei Bambini*, or "Children's House," in 1907. The concept spread like wildfire; within a year five schools had opened, and a year later the Italian-speaking part of Switzerland transformed its kindergartens into a *Casa dei Bambini*. Within a matter of a few years, the Montessori model of education had exploded; schools, societies, and literature proliferated—all based on the idea of enabling a child's natural development by providing an environment in which activities and objects supported the child's natural development and educational exploration. Montessori later called this idea "auto-education," writing in 1914 that she "did not invent a method of education—I simply gave some little children a chance to live."[21]

Montessori education also incorporates several of the solutions discussed in this book. Multi-age groups are created in the school setting, fostering an opportunity for peer support between age and ability. Children are given uninterrupted blocks of time to work and learn, while providing them guided choices from which to select. The teacher's main goals are to create an aesthetically pleasing environment and to facilitate each child's individual choice of what to focus on and learn about. Children interact with the teacher for support and guidance as needed. Students are not assigned letter grades or taught test-centric curricula, since the goal is to allow each child to excel on his or her own, rather than being put in competition against others and defining a child's success relative to the ability of his or her peers.

Whether following this method in a school environment or in the home, materials are used to enhance learning and provide tactile feedback. Sensorial materials help children use their senses to learn color, temperature, taste, size, weight, sound, etc. Practical materials are child-size tools that enable a young person to perform the work that is done in their home or community—arranging the dinner table, building materials with wood, sweeping a floor, bathing, etc. These allow children to imitate real life and build confidence and skills in the activities that adults perform on a regular basis. Academic subject materials include the same found in other school settings: books, activities, worksheets, or projects. A child's choice of what to study is respected and followed.

Montessori's list of alumni is intriguing; a disproportionately large number of graduates are innovators and disruptors of industry. Google's founders Larry Page and Sergei Brin, Amazon's founder Jeff Bezos, Wikipedia founder Jimmy Wales, and other titans of innovative industry are the products, in part, of Montessori education. Proponents of this method point to such success as evidence of Montessori's focus on helping each child develop self-awareness and motivation for learning.

HACKSCHOOLING

Logan LaPlante has been skiing the mountains near Lake Tahoe, California, since he was very young. Playing in the powdery snow is where Logan feels most alive, and what he enjoys the most. Life has been good to him, but Logan's life became much more interesting in February 2013. At the age of 13, he gave a TEDx talk to a small crowd at the University of Nevada that he expected would get no more than a thousand views.[22] It now has millions.

Logan's lecture highlighted what he called "hackschooling"—a term he coined to describe how his family allows him to customize his education. He explained that the goal of this approach is happiness, and that his pursuits are all built around that purpose. "I don't use any one particular curriculum, and I'm not dedicated to any one particular approach," Logan said in his talk. "I hack my education."[23]

The "hacker mindset" is a unique one in which systems and off-the-shelf "solutions" are fundamentally rejected; thinking outside the box is an imperative. Conventional wisdom is seen, by default, as questionable. Bruce Schneier, a computer security expert, explains this mindset:

> Hackers are as old as curiosity, although the term itself is modern. Galileo was a hacker. Madame Curie was one, too....

When I was in college, I knew a group similar to hackers: the key freaks. They wanted access, and their goal was to have a key to every lock on campus. They would study lock-picking and learn new techniques, trade maps of the steam tunnels and where they led, and exchange copies of keys with each other. A locked door was a challenge, a personal affront to their ability. These people weren't out to do damage—stealing stuff wasn't their objective—although they certainly could have. Their hobby was the power to go anywhere they wanted to....

Computer hackers follow these evolutionary lines. Or, they are the same genus operating on a new system. Computers, and networks in particular, are the new landscape to be explored. Networks provide the ultimate maze of steam tunnels, where a new hacking technique becomes a key that can open computer after computer. And inside is knowledge, understanding. Access. How things work. Why things work. It's all out there, waiting to be discovered.[24]

Education, too, is open to being hacked. Those like Logan aren't looking for perpetual revision to the existing system—they want to step away from it to come up with something better. "You never change things by fighting the existing reality," affirms the widely known saying often attributed to Buckminster Fuller, a 20th century innovator. "To change something, build a new model that makes the existing model obsolete."

Hackschooling allows Logan to learn a variety of things in a number of ways, rather than being confined to one book or one process. What does this actually look like for him? In the video Logan explains that certain subjects used to be a bore for him in the modern education system. "I didn't used to like to write," he says, "because my teachers made me write about butterflies and rainbows." He wanted to write about skiing. Focused on learning and writing about his passion, he has increased his ability and interest, and has published articles on ski enthusiast websites.

The educational freedom hackschooling allows enabled him to learn about his interests. This has resulted in Logan learning how to build skis through an internship with a ski manufacturer. He has learned about product design and sewing from interacting with employees at a baseball hat company. Most of all, hackschooling makes Logan happy.

Logan's approach to education is a new one—the idea that an entire curriculum or learning experience can be centered on a specific interest. Logan wanted to know all the ins and outs of skiing. Your child might be more fascinated by astronomy, botany, horses, computer development, video editing, or literature. Hackschooling is a way to think outside the status quo to customize and cater to your child's own path. It is, as you'll see in the next chapter, passion-driven education.

ENDNOTES

1. John Stuart Mill, *On Liberty* (Millis: Agora Publications, 2003), 130-131; punctuation and spelling has been modernized.

2. *Dead Poets Society*, Peter Weir, dir., Touchstone Pictures, 1989.

3. "A Radical Way of Unleashing a Generation of Geniuses," *Wired*, October 15, 2013, http://www.wired.com/2013/10/free-thinkers/.

4. Ibid.

5. "A whole new way of learning: Sugata Mitra's first School in the Cloud lab opens in India," *ScienceDaily*, February 4, 2014, https://www.sci-encedaily.com/releases/2014/02/140204074035.htm.

6. Daniel Greenberg, *Free at Last: The Sudbury Valley School* (Framingham: Sudbury Valley School Press, 1987), front page.

7. Ibid, 31.

8. "The school that puts kids in charge of their own education," *Deseret News National*, June 15, 2015, http://national.deseretnews.com/article/4827/the-school-that-puts-kids-in-charge-of-their-own-education.html.

9. See Peter Gray, *Free to Learn* (New York: Basic Books, 2013), 93-97.

10. Ibid.

11. *Free at Last*, 3, 5.

12. Ibid, 71.

13. Peter Gray, "The Special Value of Children's Age-Mixed Play."

14. *Free at Last*, 71.

15. Ibid, 180.

16. Thomas Paine, *The Works of Thomas Paine, vol 2*. (Philadelphia: E. Haskell, 1854), introduction.

17. "Literacy in Everyday Life: Results From the 2003 National Assessment of Adult Literacy," U.S. Department of Education, http://nces.ed.gov/Pubs2007/2007480.pdf.

18. Oliver DeMille, *A Thomas Jefferson Education* (Cedar City: George Wythe College Press, 2006), 13.

19. Letter to John Wayles Eppes, September 16, 1821, http://founders.archives.gov/documents/Jefferson/98-01-02-2317.

20. Maria Montessori, *Education and Peace* (Clio Press, 1992), 57.

21. Association Montessori Internationale, *Maria Montessori: A Centenary Anthology* (Amsterdam:Association Montessori Internationale, 1970), 27.

22. Logan LaPlante, About.me, accessed May 29, 2016, https://about.me/loganlaplante.

23. "Hackschooling makes me happy," TEDx Talks, February 12, 2013, https://www.youtube.com/watch?v=h11u3vtcpaY.

24. Bruce Schneier, *Secrets and Lies* (John Wiley & Sons, 2000), 43-44.

"A freeman ought not to be a slave in the acquisition of knowledge of any kind. Bodily exercise, when compulsory, does no harm to the body; but knowledge which is acquired under compulsion obtains no hold on the mind.

"Do not use compulsion, but let early education be a sort of amusement; you will then be better able to find out the natural bent."[1]

—PLATO

FIVE

PASSION-DRIVEN EDUCATION

s I think about my own education experience, and how it wasn't until after graduation from college that I had the freedom and mental energy to pursue a course of study that interested me, I often ponder how I can help my children experience these benefits from a young age. They should not have to suffer through drudgery for over a decade before being able to chart their own course. I want to give them a head start.

My thoughts turned to action one day when my son Keaton began peppering me with questions about Angry Birds—an extremely popular video game in which birds are flung from a slingshot and crash into various objects in an attempt to kill the pigs that are stealing their eggs. He was absorbing everything about it, developing what many parents would consider an obsession. I choose not to use that term, as it casts a child's interest in a negative light—it's a dismissive and denigrating approach to what should be considered an opportunity.

And that's how I saw it. I quickly realized that my son had handed me a silver platter onto which I could place all sorts of subjects, provided they had a tie-in to his topic of interest, Angry Birds. Passion-driven education was born.

As we've incorporated this approach into our home, I'm suddenly learning of successful people in history, as well as friends and colleagues today, who have implemented this same concept, even if they never put a name to it or articulated the reasons why they were charting this course.

I've had the opportunity to share the idea of passion-driven education with dozens of audiences around the country, and the response has been overwhelmingly positive. One stressed-out mother's comment is representative of many others I've received: "I've gone from dreading the rest of our homeschool year to absolute excitement at the thought of all of the possibilities! Thank you, thank you, thank you!"

You and your child can experience this same sense of liberation from standards, structure, and the conveyor belt by adopting a method of education that honors and embraces your child's individuality and unique interests. The goal of passion-driven education is to preserve and perpetuate the senses of awe and excitement all young children inherently have, fueling a lifelong love of learning.

HOW IT WORKS

A successful method of education must incorporate a child's interests. Children can have many interests, most of them fleeting. Quite often, however, there are one or two interests that develop into full-blown passions, where a child's mind is constantly occupied with thoughts and questions. In passion-driven education, we do not dismiss these time- and attention-consuming activities as obsessions. We see them as opportunities to infuse relevant subject matter into the process to help a child better appreciate what already interests them.

When my son began to immerse himself in Angry Birds, he did a proverbial swan dive into the deep end, learning everything he could about it. If given the opportunity, he will teach you the names of all the birds and pigs (it's a long list!), or explain the difference between the dozen or so themed Angry Birds games that exist. He is fascinated by that world and gets a sense of satisfaction and accomplishment when playing the game and achieving its objectives.

Using this passion—one that we as parents neither encouraged nor coerced—I incorporate a wide range of subject matter with a "hook" that connects it to Angry Birds. Here are a few examples, to give you insight into how passion-driven education might function:

Science. If my son flings a bird into the air, it eventually comes crashing down. Why is that? I help him understand this aspect of the game by explaining the concepts of gravity, mass, acceleration, and momentum. In the Angry Birds Space game, I can tie in lessons in astronomy. In other game variants with lush forests or desert terrain, we can talk about botany, the animal kingdom, and biomes.

Math. At the age of six, my son was doing algebra formulas that might be a struggle for kids twice his age. Rather than using abstract variables (e.g. $3X + 6 = 36$) I incorporate acronyms of the Angry Birds characters. For example, Mighty Eagle becomes ME and the equation becomes $3ME + 6 = 36$. Simply using variables tying into my son's interest engages him substantially in what otherwise might be seen as a boring and irrelevant subject of study. We also make charts and graphs plotting the number of characters used per game, or representing the various colors of each Angry Bird.

English. With only a little encouragement, Keaton began writing short stories, using Angry Birds as the protagonists. This allowed him to practice creative thinking, spelling, and penmanship, and to develop a better vocabulary. Soon, he graduated to longer stories, often using children's tales or other stories with which he is familiar, swapping out the original characters for Angry Birds. When I teach him new words, I incorporate a character or theme from the game into the sentence so that the word becomes part of the world he loves.

Creativity and Art. If you come to our home, there is a good chance you will leave with a piece of Angry Birds art of some sort. My son often illustrates the characters he loves, producing greeting cards, awards, cutouts of the birds, and other art pieces. He creates his own versions of Angry Birds-themed games, such as Sorry or chess. This allows me the opportunity to teach him about rule making, game mechanics, competition, sportsmanship, fairness, patience, etc.

Business. Contrary to how it may seem to a child, the Angry Birds app did not spontaneously come into existence. I help him understand that many people studied a long time to learn the skills necessary to work together and produce the game he loves. They formed a company, borrowed money, hired employees, bought computers and other materials, created marketing materials, and had to do hundreds of things to achieve the success that they have. I teach my son entrepreneurship through the experience of others whose products and services have benefited him.

Money. When a new Angry Birds game comes out, my son asks me if we can purchase it. I tap a button, and my credit card is charged. But what is a credit card? How is money sent from one bank to another? What, actually, is money? Why don't we use gold and silver anymore? Why do things cost more today than they did several years or decades ago? A simple app purchase opens up an entire world of commerce.

Technology. What is an app? How does a mobile device work? The technology my son uses is often taken for granted, but it provides an opportunity to explain the history of computers, coding languages, electricity, the Internet, and graphic design.

Manufacturing. My son owns Angry Birds plush toys, shirts, games, and a variety of accessories. Each of these was produced in an elaborate manufacturing process combining various natural or synthetic materials, each of which has its own origin story. With a single plush character I can teach my son about cotton production and harvesting, dyes, sewing, distribution networks, inventory management, and on and on.

Each of these subjects—and many more that can be tied in to his passion—helps my son make better sense of, and find more value in, a world he already loves. The supplementary information I share educates him, but it also empowers and emboldens his natural desire to keep learning and understanding new concepts. He is thrilled to explore every tangent and sees the learning process—when connected to his passion—as a highly enjoyable endeavor.

Parents implementing this method of education place their children's passions at the center of their educational universe. As with the other alternative methods of education, a parent can incorporate ideas and material from various curricula, websites, museums, books, videos, field trips, or other educational resources. All that's needed is a tie-in to the ideas and curiosities that consume their children's thoughts. We don't try to cram irrelevant information into children's minds—we expose them to information that helps them better understand what they are already thinking and curious about.

A completely customized curriculum, focused entirely on what has already captivated a child's mind, is based upon a simple, liberating—though rarely heeded—truth: not every person needs to know the same things, let alone all things. Obviously we want to expose children to a wide range of ideas and information both for their well-roundedness and also to help them discover new interests. But once a passion is identified—especially one that clearly will be long-lasting—it is time to allow children to deeply focus, rather than requiring them to slog through subjects that they may never use while working in their fields of interest.

For this reason, not only is passion-driven education liberating for parents who previously thought they had to assume a role of professional educator, but, more importantly, it's a freeing experience for a child no longer forced to crawl and jump through an academic obstacle course with no discernible purpose. They can forge their own path, and change at a moment's notice, ever creating their own future with the support and assistance of parents who guide them and provide resources along their journey.

There are no assignments in passion-driven education, nor are there expectations. Children are not graded by what others claim is "normal" or "standard" for their age, but are given permission to be themselves— unique people with desires, talents, and challenges that lead them to excel in some areas and struggle with others. Education occurs at the speed that best suits the individual child, which will likely vary based on the subject. Content that is more relevant to a child's passion will likely be consumed voraciously, whereas unrelated information will be sidelined or abandoned altogether. And contrary to popular belief, that is okay.

No coercion is used—only persuasion. Children are not manipulated, bribed, or pressured into learning things in which they show no interest. Parents may nudge, but they do not push; the child must always show an interest before proceeding.

Most parents in my situation would see Angry Birds as a useless distraction, a waste of time, and detrimental "screen time," instead believing that a child should be learning or playing actively outside. Treating a child's interests negatively—or even neutrally allowing them as infrequent leisure—leads to a missed opportunity to leverage that interest for the child's intellectual development and love of learning.

MORE EXAMPLES

Passion-driven education is both flexible and dynamic, always catering and adapting to the changing interests of a child. My son, for example, is not only fascinated with Angry Birds—he is likewise enthralled with LEGO and Star Wars. I use these, or any other passion he might develop, as a way to relate information to him.

In an effort to expose my children to my work—and give them an idea of what their father does with his time while he's not at home—I tell them about the meetings I have, people I speak with, or places I visit. After one morning meeting in the office, I returned home and told my children that I had met with a man who was a candidate for a state senate seat for the district in which we live.

"Just like the Galactic Senate in Star Wars!" my son said with sudden excitement.

Once again, I was given an opportunity to relate all sorts of useful information in a way that would make sense to my son. We discussed various forms of government, noting that they change over time, just as the Galactic Senate turned into the Empire. I brought up morality and ethics, basing the concepts in the code of the Jedi. The Chancellor's metamorphosis allowed me to explain a similar trend in the real world whereby people who lust for power begin to oppress others in an effort to preserve and expand it. We also spoke of war, diplomacy, rebellion, and trade agreements.

Expanding beyond that single conversation, I can use Star Wars to discuss a variety of subjects. I can bring in science by talking about charting a ship's course based on a map of stars, the vacuum of space, the speed of light, or jet propulsion. Art is an easy tie-in, with plenty of ships and planets and characters to draw on paper, model in clay, or design on the computer. I can teach math concepts by counting ships, using trigonometry to calculate the distance between the Death Star and a nearby planet, or finding the number of stormtroopers in an assembled phalanx by multiplying the number of rows and columns. Physical education already happens in our home with constant lightsaber duels and active roleplaying.

We can even use this passion in fostering a desire to learn how to play an instrument. When I was young, like many children, I was forced to practice the piano. The daily drudgery became such a conflict that once I was finally told by my parents that I could continue or quit, I didn't hesitate to choose the latter. My son, however, loves playing the piano. Why the difference? He plays Star Wars music. He is excited to master new skills and go through the necessary lessons so he can improve and better be able to play the tunes he is constantly humming throughout the day. He also plays the cello, and can barely contain his happiness when he learns how to play a new part of a Star Wars song.

Any topic is on the table, and can be used to weave in interesting information and insights to which a child might not otherwise be exposed. Let's consider how this approach to education might look with a variety of other passions. (*If you want to skip these detailed examples, continue reading on the bottom of page 143.*)

Horses. *History*: learn about world events through the perspective of the horses being used to pull carriages, fight in battles, etc.; find out which breeds were preferred by which groups of people and for what purpose; introduce historical figures who used horses; analyze socio-economic changes that affected what classes of people could afford a horse. *English*: write short stories about horses being used in different epochs of world history; read books on horse behavior or how to raise one; submit an essay to a horse-related magazine. *Science*: use a horse's diet to learn about calories, fat, vitamins, and nutrition; discuss mating, reproduction, and nature vs. nurture; study hereditary genetics and differences between various horse breeds; teach about pigment and compare horse hair to human hair using a microscope. *Math*: compile population estimates of horses in different countries and chart them over time;

use a horse's body to introduce concepts like mass, volume, and density; calculate the amount of time it would take a horse to travel various distances. *Art and creativity*: provide modeling clay to create a sculpture of a horse; introduce graphic design in order to animate a galloping horse; encourage roleplaying by providing broomstick horses, costumes, and other props.

Cooking. *History*: study how people's diets have changed over time, and why; learn about how people have harvested and preserved food in the past; review different wars by studying the diets of soldiers; read about pioneers and pilgrims to determine what they ate and how they cooked while on the move. *English*: create recipe cards for favorite dishes; start a blog to share cooking secrets and document progress; read recipes and write a shopping list; keep a food journal documenting daily intake and reviewing each item's qualities. *Science*: learn about chemical reactions and how they can affect food; introduce the Kingdoms of Life using the foods we eat; investigate food technology and recent inventions used to increase the nutritional quality and shelf life of food; discuss temperature, altitude, humidity, and their effects on cooking. *Math*: learn about various units of measure and how they are used when cooking; calculate the cost of each meal by pricing ingredients and measuring how much is used in the meal; discuss volume and weight by measuring jars of spices; cut pieces of lunchmeat into various shapes to introduce geometry and trigonometry. *Art and creativity*: compete with parents or siblings to create the most colorful dessert; teach cursive and calligraphy to create a fancy meal invitation for family or friends; practice painting using only dyes or juices from food.

Minecraft. *History*: create buildings of historical significance and learn about the culture and beliefs of the people who built them; build battlefields and internment camps to discuss the ethics of war and the justice of past military campaigns; make ships, trains, and trucks and discuss the changes in distribution of commerce through history. *English*: provide journal prompts that can be used to document what happened during each game; author a detailed guide or walkthrough that can be used to teach a friend or sibling how to play Minecraft; write a creative backstory about each character designed in the game. *Science*: explain electrical engineering using the doors, buttons, levers, and other contraptions present in the game; discuss architecture, structural integrity, scale modeling, and measurements while creating buildings; use a Minecraft house's surroundings to discuss ecology, environmental science, weather patterns, etc.; create a model of DNA and discuss biology. *Math*: teach concepts like volume, area, and perimeter using blocks and buildings; use Google's plugin that lets the user experience quantum physics; provide opportunities to build problem-solving skills, such as: With 26 arrows to fight off an approaching group of four skeletons, how many arrows can you use on each skeleton? *Art and creativity*: using construction paper and other art supplies, create a physical replica of a virtual Minecraft environment; create an Olympics or other athletic contest in which the characters may compete.

Animals. *History*: learn about cultures that have treated animals as deities; teach the various epochs of world history by reviewing a list of extinct species and the causes of their demise; use the predator/prey relationship to discuss the dominance of weak nations by more powerful nations. *English*: create a theatrical production where each family member has a supporting role and the family pet has the lead role; write short stories about a world without humans, where animals at the top of the food chain rule over those at the lower end; keep a daily journal about the eating habits, behaviors, and physical activities of a family pet; volunteer at a shelter or zoo and write a series of blog posts about the experience. *Science*: learn about binomial nomenclature and how animals are formally named; discuss anatomy by dissecting a frog, worm, or other animal or insect; discuss the theory of evolution and how animals adapt to their environment. *Math*: teach statistics by analyzing the population changes of various animals or their relative population in each part of the world; introduce algebra using different animals as variables; practice estimating and rounding by quickly counting groups of animals in the wild (or in an online video).

Art and creativity: create animal sock puppets; learn woodworking to build a bird feeder; build clay models of favorite animals; design an elaborate obstacle course for a family pet.

Cars. *History*: learn about the various methods of transportation before the combustion engine was invented; study the inventors who designed each component of a car and the circumstances that led to the innovation; use toy cars to recreate epic battle scenes and discuss the grievances that led to them. *English*: compose short stories about what ancient cultures might have been like if cars existed at the time; create a daily driving journal describing how far the family drove, where to, and why; write explanations of how to perform basic car maintenance that can be shared with a younger sibling or friend. *Science*: learn about potential and kinetic energy and how they apply to a vehicle; create a controlled combustion experiment to learn how an engine works; introduce physics using a vehicle to discuss concepts such as motion, linear momentum, torque, and thermodynamics; analyze the components in gasoline and how it is extracted and processed from oil. *Math*: review probability and statistics using data about car accidents; use vehicle components to introduce geometric concepts; explain differential calculus in the context of an accelerating car. *Art and creativity*: build cars out of LEGO; creatively paint an abandoned or junked car; learn Adobe Illustrator to create digital paintings of favorite vehicles.

LEGO. *History*: build historical buildings and learn about the people who created and used them; use LEGO people to represent different countries interacting with, or fighting against, one another throughout history; create ships and trains and carriages and other modes of transportation to discuss how technology and travel have changed throughout time. *English*: create a script for family members to act out a play using LEGO characters; write a letter to the manufacturers of LEGO suggesting a new design or theme; after assembling a castle or house, write a short story using it as the setting. *Science*: learn how plastic is made; create a periodic table using LEGO to teach chemistry; use LEGO animals and plants to discuss biology; learn about weight, lift, thrust, and drag using LEGO airplanes; create mountains and hills using blocks to learn about topography, elevation, soil erosion, etc. *Math*: introduce fractions by using the different sizes of LEGO to represent parts of a whole; teach geometry using the shapes and sizes of LEGO; explore differential calculus by plotting LEGO curves on a coordinate graph created with blocks. *Art and creativity*: create custom instructions to help a sibling or friend learn how to assemble something unique; build a model version of your home; create a Rube Goldberg machine using LEGO.

Dance. *History*: practice popular dances from different countries and learn about the symbolism in the dances; research cultures that prohibited dancing; study artifacts showing how ancient civilizations viewed dancing. *English*: create a series of fictional short stories about a protagonist who uses professional dancing as a cover for his or her secret spy activities; write a letter to the editor about the cultural importance of dancing and submit it to your local newspaper; read books that discuss different dancing techniques. *Science*: use the motions of dance to discuss angular momentum, gravity, force, and related concepts; look into dance science programs that teach physiology, anatomy, kinesiology, psychology, biomechanics, nutrition, and similar fields of study. *Math*: choreograph a dance using geometric shapes; use dancing stick figures in place of variables in algebra formulas; teach about angles or trigonometry using dance positions with extended arms or legs. *Art and creativity*: perform an interpretative dance that represents the personality of each person in the family; organize a dance competition for friends and neighbors; start an online video course teaching others how to dance.

This approach to education encourages parents to see each subject as a different organ of a body, with a child's passion serving as the connective tissue holding them together. Passion-driven education should be broad in scope. If my son develops a passion for aviation, his education can—and should—focus narrowly on that interest. Yet, as part of that interest, he would need to learn math, physics, aeronautics, mechanical engineering, communications, manufacturing, and other aspects involved in making and flying a plane. Ultimately, he would likely decide to specialize in one aspect of the field, but his broader background in fields related to aviation would provide proper context for his particular area of interest. Similarly, video gamers might learn computer development in order to create their own games, or dancers could study music theory to help them excel in the sport.

For older children, this means helping them obtain internships in their particular interest so they can spend a significant amount of time immersed in the field. An internship exposes them to mentors and professionals who are experienced in that subject and who provide accountability; rather than learning what they want at a pace they prefer, interns have to fulfill obligations in a real-world setting, preparing them for the rigors of meeting other's needs and expectations. If successful, an internship provides an excellent leap forward into a career, with a new network of colleagues and work experience that translate into opportunity.

Following a passion for its own sake is the ideal of this method of learning, but how that works varies with time and experience. Exposing our children to different subjects, especially in their earlier years, helps them to become well-rounded and introduces them to ideas they may find interesting and relevant to their future paths, but more importantly, it allows us to focus on their specific interests later on. A child's passion becomes both educational and experiential—in other words, they learn about and directly participate in the very things they love.

CHALLENGES AND CONCERNS

As I've presented the idea of passion-driven education to audiences around the country, a few questions consistently come up from parents who have clearly become intrigued, yet who have a lingering doubt or particular circumstance in their life that might make the idea difficult to implement. Answering each of them here will hopefully enable you to gain the confidence to formulate a more detailed plan of action.

How does passion-driven education work with young children? Perhaps you noticed that the examples I shared from our own home featured only our son. He has a younger sister who, like many young children, doesn't quite have any passions of her own. She is also interested in Angry Birds and Star Wars like her brother, yet probably has those interests because she wants to be like, and around, her brother—not because they are genuinely her own. Still, we can introduce her to new information using these interests. With very young children the important idea is to always treat learning as interesting and enjoyable. It may not be connected to a deeply held passion quite yet, but that's okay. Our focus is to preserve and augment their natural love of learning so it continues to grow as they do.

Can focusing too much on a passion become detrimental? Anything taken to an extreme can be a problem. Children's interests are a positive thing when they stimulate thinking and engage their minds. If they become the focus of attention to the exclusion of all else— if relationships suffer, chores aren't being completed, productivity drops to zero, etc.—then it may be time to appropriately intervene, set some boundaries, or encourage alternative activities. It's important to reason with children, explain the consequences for their choices, and let them participate in determining a responsible way to manage their interests such that they do not detract from other important aspects of life. A positive passion can become a negative obsession if life balance is lost.

How do I start passion-driven education in my home? Parents who once relied on curricula to structure their efforts often recognize the importance of education freedom but find it intimidating. Starting passion-driven education is easy: simply listen to your children. Let them choose what the two of you spend time on each day. If your children struggle to develop any ideas, then help research five ideas, discuss the pros and cons of each, and let them pick. Give your children more ownership of their day, and be observant about what they respond to and show interest in. Resist the urge to compare your children to others or feel like they should be held to an arbitrary standard dictating what they should know at which age. Enjoy life together, discover learning opportunities in everything you do, and slowly encourage your children to take advantage of their freedom by planning what material they want to learn and what educational experiences they want to create.

How do I transition my child from public school to passion-driven education? Embracing an alternative mindset can be difficult, especially for parents who are the byproduct of generations of public schooling. Families making the transition from the modern education system to any alternative method (not just passion-driven education) should consider de-schooling: a period of time allocated to adjust to learning in an unstructured environment. A common recommendation is to de-school one month for every year of schooling. For example, parents of a fourth grader being removed from school would spend four months de-schooling. During this period of time, try to avoid anything that comes across as school-ish: textbooks, worksheets, formal instruction, etc. Think of every weekday as a Saturday; plan enriching activities and spend time together. Find learning opportunities in everything you do, but keep the education informal and interesting. This process is at least as important for the parents as it is for the child, providing both of you a smooth transition into an alternative education format that will look radically different from what you have been used to.

What if my children have no passions? It may take time for your children to settle on something around which you can create a custom curriculum. For now, focus on what matters to them—even if it's a fleeting curiosity. Observe what catches their attention and gently provide interesting tangential information. The important thing is to not force anything. Expose them to material from a broad range of topics, and if you meet resistance in one area, back off for a while and consider a new approach at a later date. A serious passion may not develop until a later age. In the meantime, you can still provide interesting educational opportunities and expose your children to a wide range of material.

Do I have to homeschool in order to do passion-driven education? The freedom required of this education model lends itself best to a homeschool or unschool environment, where structure is absent and children are provided the flexibility to deeply follow their curiosities, wherever they may lead. However, not all families are able to accommodate this and, therefore, adaptation is necessary. Passion-driven education is possible in more structured environments, though it will not be realized to its fullest degree. Children required to attend high school will have limited time and mental energy outside of class time, homework, and test preparation, to explore other interests. However, Bill Gates, Steve Jobs, Oprah Winfrey, and Mark Zuckerberg are all famous examples of highly successful people who actively pursued their passions in their personal time while finishing their time in a traditional high school setting. Weekends, vacations, and summer breaks can be utilized to encourage children to focus on their passions and learn about different subjects. Parents in this situation should work to establish an expectation that education is a year-long endeavor, and is not limited to the school schedule; vacations and school breaks are not an excuse to turn off one's brain.

Is passion-driven education hands-off? Letting children follow their passion does not imply permission to engage in destructive behavior. For example, a love of music does not mean a child should be allowed to attend a rave. A passion for literature does not mean a child should be allowed to read inappropriate material. Allowing more freedom for children does not mean that they are adults; parents should still parent. Do not feel like you should say yes to what your children ask merely because their request has a connection to their passion. Be judicious and provide your children only with what is beneficial for them.

How much do I have to be involved in my children's daily learning? Young child are going to need significant support. Parents practicing passion-driven education will be focused on paying attention to their ever-changing interests and exposing them to different ideas and information. As children mature and become more independent, parents allow them to focus narrowly and deeply on their passion—one about which, in many cases, the parent knows very little. During these teenage years a parent may not be as directly involved in the education process, yet is no less busy. Passion-driven education has different demands of a parent in this situation, such as helping plan trips, brainstorming ideas for an entrepreneurial venture, recruiting mentors for their children, driving a child to an internship, etc. As a general rule, parents should be as involved as the child allows them—as a facilitator partnering with them to follow their unique path in life.

Can advanced topics be taught using passion-driven education? The main goal behind this approach to learning is to expose a child to a wide variety of topics that without context would be seen as boring or irrelevant. For that reason, much of the information might be at an introductory level. However, a secondary purpose of passion-driven education is to generate a deep interest in the new subject matter being introduced. For example, parents of a child who is passionate about planes might introduce videography by taking the child to an air show and encouraging him or her to create a short documentary about the experience. That "hook" might create an interest in video editing, sparking a desire to master that skill and launch a lucrative career providing the service to others. Passion-driven education focuses on a child's current interests when introducing new information, recognizing that one or more of those topics may itself become a new passion.

Will my child get into college? Many colleges are eager to admit homeschooled youth, recognizing that they are often more ambitious and well-rounded than their public school peers. Most teenagers applying to college report no difficulty in being admitted, and those who sidestep the modern education system have plenty of ways to demonstrate their knowledge and abilities during the admission process. Take note, however, that passion-driven education may lead to an alternative path outside of higher education; a child is more likely to start their own business and dive into his or her field of interest than to sit behind a desk for several years and incur significant debt.

Keep in mind that passion-driven education is no guarantee that a child's life will be a steady stream of enthusiasm and excitement. As with anything, there are peaks and valleys; interests come and go and sometimes are altogether absent. As parents, we need to practice the very flexibility that we are providing for our children, always being able and willing to adapt to their changing interests. The goal is, and always must be, to keep our children curious.

FEAR OF FREEDOM

Passion-driven education does not work without an increased amount of freedom for children to pursue and study their interests. It's this very freedom that terrifies many parents. The reasons why are obvious. We who are products of the modern education system are accustomed to authoritarianism and structure. We doubt our ability to adapt to an alternative method and philosophy. We're worried about what family or friends will think about our going against the grain and taking a radically different approach. And deep down, we want our children to fit in and, notwithstanding its problems, be on the conveyor belt so as to not be left behind or miss out on what other children are experiencing.

These fears are understandable and common. Each should be addressed thoughtfully and rationally. In deciding to explore an alternative path, you need courage in your convictions and the ability to articulate the reasons why you are abandoning the modern education system. This book helps provide that ammunition, but to fully embrace passion-driven education you will need to do more than merely respond to fear. You will need to have faith.

Children are naturally curious and stricken with a sense of awe about the world in which they live. They have personality traits, talents, interests, and inclinations that drive them down a path that is uniquely their own. Have faith that they have a purpose in life that you do not know—and that they do not yet know, either. Consider that your children's happiness and potential will be found along a path of their own discovery, rather than a standardized conveyor belt. Have faith that your children's very nature carries with it an internal motivation to put their unique imprint upon the world, and that just as a seed germinates into a plant with the proper resources, your children will thrive if supplied with what they need.

Have faith in your children and their natural ability to flourish. Have faith that you, as a parent, will be able to recognize their passions and conjure up ideas that will expand their awareness and entice them to learn more. Have faith in your natural ability to rear and care for your child—not as a source of information or an authoritarian teacher, but as a nurturer and provider of necessary and helpful resources. Have faith that you can walk this path with your child without exclusively relying on the crutch of an off-the-shelf curriculum to support you. Acting in faith will yield positive results over time, which will resolve your fears far better than a list of pros and cons.

Like many parents who implement an alternative education method and allow their children to follow their passions, Teresa Bondora worried about her children constantly. Her daughter was "obsessed" with everything Disney and would spend countless hours watching the movies, going to the Disney Store, and researching random, "useless" facts until "she became an encyclopedia," able to tell you any factoid imaginable about the characters and stories.[2] "The history of Walt himself, his brother Roy, what the numbers on the doors on Main Street meant, the Google Earth view, the roads there, YouTube videos on abandoned things, what happened to the parts of the 20,000 Leagues ride. I mean, seriously, deep into details of everything." Teresa explains her fears:

> This went on for years and I secretly worried that while she was a good reader and knew a lot of stuff about a lot of stuff, she wasn't really doing anything that resembled anything like working toward any career or skill. I saw visions of her with kids, being left a single mom and not one skill to support herself. Or maybe she was going to live with me until she was 30. Or maybe she'd move out and back in repeatedly. Then she told me, she wanted to work at Disney World. "Great", I thought. "A part-time, minimum wage job pushing a button on a ride."

Meanwhile, Teresa's son developed an interest in Minecraft and played "All. The. Time." As her son stared at a screen and her daughter saved her money for an annual pass to Disney World instead of college, Teresa's fears took over. "My unschooling experiment was failing right in front of my eyes," she said, "but this was their entire life that I was failing." With a dream of working at Disney World in order to live her passion, Teresa's daughter moved to Florida and found a job in retail, which she soon quit to explore Disney World in more detail and figure out a way to get a job there. Teresa got a phone call with the news, and it didn't go well.

> I hung up and cried. I cried so much. I worried so much because now, *now* when the reality of not having any money, no job, and being unable to pay rent sinks in, she will come home broken and I will have to sit down and apologize for failing her in the most profound way a mother could ever fail her child.

But that didn't happen. Her daughter secured an interview, performed well, and got a job. "And in that moment," Teresa said, "I burst into tears for all the years of fear and terror and sadness and worry and all the joy any mother could feel. And in that moment I knew that she knew she was always okay." Her daughter's dream has come true, and she has moved up the ranks of the Disney empire, impressing visitors and her superiors with her comprehensive knowledge. The work paid off for her, even though at the time it did not seem like work—it felt, to Teresa, like an obsession taking time away from basic academics and other areas of interest that seemed to guarantee a better chance of future success.

And her Minecraft-obsessed son? He learned about chemistry as a result of his gaming and now wants to study astrophysics. He and Teresa are co-writing a book on the chemistry of Minecraft. While he requested to be homeschooled, he decided he wanted to follow the structure used in high school to prepare for the SAT exam. Teresa points out that following a formal curriculum was her son's choice, and that's what matters. "Together we will forge a future into the unknown, one day at a time," she says. "And as one lucky mom, I get to play in the playgrounds of my children's creation. What more could a mother ask for?"

Our goal as parents should be to help our children discover their paths as soon as possible, understanding that when it is found, their excitement and ambition will skyrocket. We won't have to harass them about homework and coerce them to learn. If anything, we'll be incessantly reminding them to fulfill basic personal and household duties before they immerse themselves in their passion for the day. Education changes from drudgery to a delight. A child's attitude toward learning becomes what it once was as a young child: wonderful, in the true sense of the word.

Children's passions provide a tremendous opportunity to help them discover and pursue their path in life.

These passions are the ideas that resonate with their soul and augment their sense of wonder. They allow us to speak to our children in a language they already know and love. Providing our children with the freedom and time to focus on their passions honors their individuality and validates their positive choices. It allows them to be themselves, rather than saying and doing what others tell them.

Implementing passion-driven education brings with it significant potential for your children's internal motivation, quality of life, and future success. On the other hand, a failure to provide them the time and freedom to follow their interests carries significant risk. If we fear allowing our children to focus deeply on what they care about the most, we effectively introduce parental roadblocks in their life paths that may not be surmounted for years, if ever. What would our world be like today if John D. Rockefeller, Walt Disney, Henry Ford, Frank Sinatra, and thousands of other famous and successful pioneers of industry and culture had been prevented from departing the modern education system to focus on their passions? What is our world missing out on today, in terms of untapped potential, because would-be innovators, entrepreneurs, philosophers, or philanthropists are being dumbed down through force-fed material day after day, suppressing and sapping their mental energy and love of learning?

What will *your* children miss out on if not given the freedom to follow their passions?

Catalog your fears and address them head on. Find experienced parents who can mentor and reassure you. And have faith—faith in freedom's potential to accelerate your child's education far beyond where it would otherwise be; faith that allowing your children to spend their time focused on the things that matter to them will lead to a meaningful and happy life; and faith that this journey will remove stress, contention, and coercion from your home. Most importantly, have faith that passion-driven education will ignite in your child a lifelong love of learning.

It has worked for children of all ages in families throughout history and around the world. It can work for yours.

ENDNOTES

1. Plato, *The Republic and Other Works* (New York: Anchor Books, 1973), 229.

2. "Interviews with Homeschoolers," Juli Gauthier, http://www.juligauthier.com/blog/2016/2/14/ interviews-with-homeschoolers-2. Teresa has given permission to the author to include her story here.

CONCLUSION

‒‒‒‒‒‒‒‒‒‒‒‒‒‒‒‒‒‒‒‒

Randall Lee Church was sentenced to prison in 1983 for fatally stabbing a man. He claims it was in self-defense—the result of a drunken fight over $97 that went downhill quickly—but he failed to persuade the jury. 1983 may seem like a world away for those of us who have lived productive lives in the meantime. It was the year President Reagan labeled the Soviet Union the "Evil Empire" as the Cold War escalated. Microsoft Word 1.0 was released that year, and the first CD player had been invented just a few months earlier.

While these milestones seem like another lifetime to you and me, it is the only world that Church relates to and knows. Released in 2011, he couldn't adjust to a society that had moved on without him. "Everything had gone fast forward without me,"[1] he said in an interview. Just three months of freedom was enough to convince him that he couldn't handle it. He wanted to go back to prison.

Church burned down a house to make it happen.

Not every released convict wants to return to prison, but many struggle with their newfound freedom. "There are a lot of people who do not want to go back to jail," said a prison chaplain. "They want to do the right thing, but they don't know how. They don't know how to be free people. In prison you learn life values that are useless in the real world."[2]

It must be an odd experience to abruptly switch from imprisonment to freedom. Yet this is precisely what happens at the conclusion of one's time in the modern education system, where millions of children reach the end of the conveyor belt and wonder what to do next. They, too, have learned information that is "useless in the real world" and struggle to succeed on their own. And the comparison between school and prison is, sadly, a valid one. In both institutions, the subjects must navigate an extremely authoritarian system: emphasis is placed on obedience and order; a dress code must be followed; individual autonomy is largely prohibited; schedules are micro-managed; permission is required to use the restroom; no input is allowed for any decision making; and those who break a rule are swiftly punished. Students and prisoners alike are rewarded for "good" behavior, conditioning them to do what they are told, rather than what they desire. Individual identity is diminished.

Arguably, that type of treatment may be proper for a criminal, but it's hardly ideal for a child. Young people should be transitioned gradually into adulthood and equipped with knowledge and skills that will maximize their opportunity for success and happiness. They should experience more freedom as they mature and learn—not in one sudden stroke upon graduation from school. A child shouldn't be made to feel like Randall Lee Church, disoriented and unsettled by suddenly becoming unchained. We don't want our children to long for the conformity and control of an authoritarian system. Schools breed submissive adults who are deferential to authority figures and unable to think critically and act accordingly. The state of our society provides too many examples of this sad truth.

As important as it is in a child's educational experience, recognizing that one can opt for freedom from the standard education model is only a first step—as if a door has been placed adjacent to the conveyor belt, beckoning children to step into a portal leading to a different world. The second step is choosing to take advantage of that freedom. Having a choice is important, but what matters more is what choice is made.

Caring parents must consider the environments and circumstances in which their children will be placed, and the resulting challenges and influences that will affect those choices. Placing a child in a government school may be convenient, but it carries tremendous risk. Educating children in the home may require the sacrifice of time and energy, but it enables families to avoid the problems associated with the modern education system. And passion-driven education, more than any of the available alternatives, provides children with choices that are interesting and relevant to them.

What daily activities will help a child excel in life? What curriculum should be used, if any? Should a child be required to learn a specific set of facts, figures, and formulas? What will preserve (or resurrect) a child's natural desire to learn? These are questions that too many parents do not thoughtfully consider. Often, parents expect school administrators and teachers to ask and answer such questions and ensure a successful outcome for their child. Look at the product of the modern education system—typically, an apathetic teenager drifting aimlessly through life with little ambition or awareness of how the world operates. Is that what you want for your child?

A popular kids' game show, *Runaround*, aired on TV in the early 1970s. Children would huddle together on the studio floor, awaiting a question. Once it was asked, the host would shout "Runaround!" and the young contestants would quickly group together in one of three zones, each representing a potential answer to the question. On many occasions the children would be unsure of an answer, and would watch to see where the other competitors were going before desperately launching themselves in the same direction.

Successful contestants were strategic enough to avoid the herd mentality and make the best choice they could.

While a majority of parents entrust their children's most formative developmental years to the modern education system, unaware of or uninterested in the problems it introduces, you don't have to follow them. Chances are, much like the young players on *Runaround*, they have no clue what the answers are. They are just doing what everybody else is doing, thinking it's the right answer.

Think different.

I look back on my youth and realize how in many ways, schooling snuffed out my interest in education. The results of thousands of hours of sitting in a classroom include profoundly wasted time, misdirected energy, and lost opportunity. As a father, the thought of my children having the same experience terrifies me. While I can't alter my past, I can try to not subject my children to the same ordeal. I can leverage their personal passions to expose them to a wide range of information and issues that excite and empower them. I can be like a farmer providing resources and nutrients to a young plant looking to establish a strong root system. I can provide my children the educational freedom I never had, enabling them to take ownership of their future. I can ignite within them a lifelong love of learning.

You can, too.

ENDNOTES

1. "Convict couldn't handle being free," *San Antonio Express-News*, September 25, 2011, http://www.mysanantonio.com/news/local_news/article/Convictcouldn-thandlebeing-free-2187648.php.
2. Yvonne Y. Haddad, Farid Senzai, Jane I. Smith, *Educating the Muslims of America* (Oxford University Press, 2009).

THANK YOU FOR READING!

Dear Reader,

May I ask you a favor? I am anxious to get this book into as many hands as possible. One of the easiest ways you can help is simply by sharing your thoughts about the book with others.

Please go to **TinyUrl.com/PDEreview** to leave a review of the book on Amazon.com. Your review helps promote the book by elevating it in the rankings for potential customers to see.

If you *really* liked the book, please also consider recommending it to friends and family on your favorite social networking site or via email. You are my marketing team!

I hope this information has been both motivational and practical for you, inspiring a positive change in your parenting efforts.

Sincerely,

THE TUTTLE TWINS

Each year, hundreds of millions of children are spoon-fed false history, bad economics, and logical fallacies. *Your child is not immune.*

Well meaning parents have long desired a way to inoculate their children against this trend to help them really grasp the importance of freedom and free markets—the pillars of good government that made America great.

These parents—just like you—have had nowhere to turn, and no literature to provide their child... **until now**! The solution is here: The Tuttle Twins books.

Get the books—with a discount and freebies—at:
TuttleTwins.com

INDEX

ABOUT THE AUTHOR

Connor Boyack is founder and president of Libertas Institute, a free market think tank in Utah. In that capacity, he has spearheaded important policy reforms dealing with education reform, parental rights, property rights, civil liberties, transparency, and surveillance.

He is the author of ten books covering issues such as politics, religion, and education. His award-winning The Tuttle Twins series teaches the principles of liberty to young children.

Connor's work has been publicly praised by many nationally recognized figures, and he frequently appears in local, national, and international interviews to publicize and comment on his work.

Connor lives in Utah with his wife and two children.

Find all of Boyack's books for sale at LibertasUtah.org/shop/